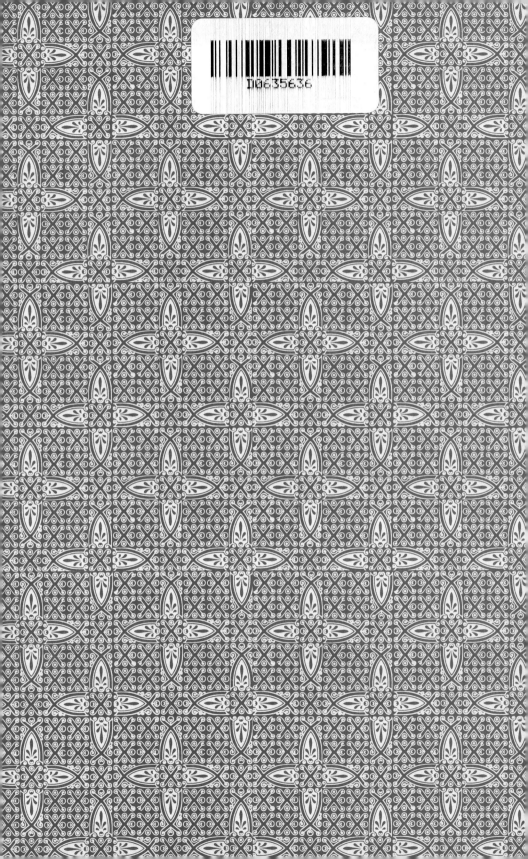

Travels in the
South of France

# Stendhal

## Travels in the South of France

Translated by Elisabeth Abbott

Introduction by Victor Brombert

Calder & Boyars · London

Other works by Stendhal published by Calder & Boyars

*Haydn, Mozart and Metastasio*
*Life of Rossini*
*Rome, Naples and Florence*
*Selected Journalism*

*First published in Great Britain in 1971*
*by Calder & Boyars Ltd.*
*18 Brewer Street London W1*
*© Elisabeth Abbott 1970*
*© Introduction, Victor Brombert 1970*
*All rights reserved*
*ISBN 0 7145 0818 7*
*Printed by Halliday Lithograph Corp., West Hanover, Mass.*

# ·⊰[ Contents ]⊱·

# ·⇥⟨ *Introduction* ⟩⇤·

Stendhal would certainly have been pleased to learn that his unassuming *Travels in the South of France* could, over a century later, be read as social history. Not that these pages offer any theoretical development or even any systematic analyses. Stendhal, by temperament, prefers the digressive, even the flippant comment; he moves with speed from one observation to another, rarely on the same level, often with conscious irrelevance. Yet the reader, curious about travel conditions in mid-century France, about the distinctive characteristics of certain towns and regions, about social classes and their fluidity, will find here some interesting and amusing observations. Eating habits at the *table d'hôte*, the unpleasant paving stones in Toulouse, the quality of water in various cities, how people make a fortune in Bordeaux, the cost of travel and hotels, digressions on politics and regional myths—all these are thrown pell-mell. Sometimes, as when the inhabitants of Marseille are praised for their reliability and plain, sober speech, the reader can also measure the distance that separates certain myths or clichés of the 19th century and of our own period. Stendhal who is always fascinated by historical evolution and relativism would certainly also have been pleased to know that his text provides this kind of perspective.

It is hardly surprising that so many incidental details, such sporadic writing, such fondness for disconnected anecdotes, should not be conducive to a unified or even structured work. The Stendhalian qualities are obvious: incisive cultural diagnoses, comparisons between Paris and the Provinces (an important dialectical factor in his novels), anti-clerical sallies, typical allusions to his private sentimental life. Only the initiated Stendhal fan will understand the full meaning of passing references to Angela Pietragrua (the easy-virtued Milanese who betrayed him), to Count Daru, his early protector, to Mathilde Dembowski, the inaccessible lady he would never forget, to the Italian interlude of 1814–1821 when he frequented the Carbonaro activists. None of this, of course, has anything to do with travels in the south of France. But that is how Stendhal enjoyed writing, especially when he settled down to what was an "alimentary" literary exercise. The more commercial the enterprise, the more he delighted in transforming it into an intensely private affair.

The egocentric stance of the tourist writing about his travels for a potential but unknown audience lent itself to such ambiguities.

Taken objectively, the book as it now stands is likely to surprise the reader who expects echoes of the *Red and the Black* and the *Charterhouse of Parma*. The chief concern of this traveler-writer seems, in every town he explores, to find a café with good service. But then the book as it stands never really existed; what we have here are notes toward a book. Moreover that unwritten book would, in our day and age, be an anomaly; much of its substance—for instance the precise measurements of given works of architecture as well as useful addresses —would now be sought in the *Guide Bleu*, the *Guide Michelin*, or their equivalents. Tourism was in its infancy, and it must be remembered that Stendhal is largely responsible, in France at least, for the very word and concept.

*Travels in the South of France*, for which Stendhal set out on a partly documentary, partly hedonistic journey, can be considered as a companion to his recently completed *Memoirs of a Tourist*. In March of 1838, Henri Beyle-Stendhal, the French Consul in the Papal City of Civitavecchia (often absent from his post, or on prolonged leaves in France!) left for the Provinces. He traveled for over four months, visiting Bordeaux, Toulouse, Pau, Marseille, Toulon, Geneva, Cannes, Valence. He returned to Paris in late July, by way of Switzerland, Germany and Holland. Some of these places he knew well—Marseille for instance, where many years earlier he had followed an actress. These travel notes do not, however, extend beyond May 22. What we have here is a rough first draft, some first impressions, with all the inevitable redundancies, gaps to be filled later, developments to be woven into the basic outline. For the student of Stendhal, these five notebooks, now in the Grenoble public library, provide an insight into Stendhal's method of composition. They cast light on the point of encounter of an acute sensibility with an artificial labor that has not quite become a work.

For a general reader or student of literature there are other problems, some of them far-reaching. What is that curious "genre" of travel books, what need does it fulfill? What is its origin, its relation to the mainstream of literature? How private, how public-oriented is it? What for instance impels a Président des Brosses, whom Stendhal admired greatly, to write his Italian letters for his friends? Why is it that the 18th century, with which Stendhal has so many ties, delights particularly in travel accounts? What clientele does the genre satisfy, and is there a relation between social evolution and the desire to see other places? Can one establish a parallel between the cultural relativism of the Age of Enlightenment and the personal pleasure taken in moving from town to town, from region to region, from country to country? The subject easily assumes sociological and even anthropological dimensions. What is it—especially in modern times—that impels people to travel? Is it a new form of quest, a new and totally lay form of pilgrimage?

Surely simple sensationalism is too easy an answer. The taste for change, for the exotic, for the elsewhere, corresponds to deeper needs of the spirit. Even in the crassest travel advertisements of our day there can be found suggestions of loftier needs: adventure, discovery, revelation. Mobility may appear as a manifestation of restlessness, as a desire to escape. Yet it also points to other symptoms: the search for a hidden truth, the refusal to be satisfied, the belief that even the trivial can have hidden meaning, and that topographic displacement, instead of releasing the self from the self, brings about a closer awareness of one's identity. Pascal, it is true, inveighed against the need for distraction; according to him, nothing could be deadlier than man's inability to face up to himself in the monastic silence of his own room. He diagnosed the *horreur du domicile* as a fundamental spiritual disease. Nonetheless, ever since antiquity (even Christian symbolism stresses the "voyage"), travel has been symbolically synonymous with a lesson, an education, or better still an initiation into a secret. Ultimately, life itself has taken on the metaphoric figuration of a journey. The image of Telemachus is in a sense exemplary, not only because he is to look for his identity by way of a father-search, but because in more recent treatments (Balzac, Joyce) this search takes place against the huge backdrop of the metropolis, thus pointing to a specific poetic view of the modern city. The Aragon of the Surrealist years understood this perfectly, when, by a paradoxical twist, he entitled one of his most brilliant texts *Le Paysan de Paris*.

Are we getting far away from Stendhal? Perhaps—if we limit our reading to what the text literally tells us, if we remain at the level of what Stendhal says he sees. There, at best, the statistical and anecdotal elements are transcended only on such occasions when the author draws parallels between art and politics, or when he becomes passionate and partial. (Bias is indeed one of Stendhal's strong points.) But the text takes on an altogether different significance as soon as one becomes attuned to the specific hedonism involved, which no amount of dryness can disguise. Then the unassuming and ironic lyricism comes through, as clear and yet as muted as the evening bells Stendhal loved to hear in unknown cities, and which for him had the profound charm of a presage or an invitation. How different from the metaphysical serious-ness and even gloom with which Flaubert approached the whole matter of travel. For Stendhal, the intense joys of traveling are never orgiastic; they do not imply a morbid quest for the absolute, an almost self-destructive drive. To enter new cities, to return to beloved places, to try out a restaurant, to look at strange faces in unfamiliar streets and to imagine how these people go about seeking happiness (the famous *chasse au bonheur*)—these are for him liberating activities. Travel is here the counterpart of that freeing anonymity that Stendhal sought in the act of writing.

The very love of pseudonyms—Stendhal is but the most famous among several dozens—suggests an intellectual masquerade. Just as the pseudonym is an act of emancipation and even protest (the father being thereby rejected), so also the pleasure of touring foreign countries or provinces is a manner of declaration of independence vis-à-vis one's origin. And so is writing—and in particular the weaving of fiction—a way of wearing a liberating and self-creating mask. Stendhal was moreover well aware of the intimate link between travel and the passion to write—and for that matter all "passion". In an allusion to Dominique (another pseudonym), he confesses his happiness to have passion as a profession!

The works in which tourism, in one form or another, plays a central role, are almost more numerous than his fictional constructs. Or rather, they tend to merge. *Rome, Naples and Florence in 1817* uses the pseu-donym Stendhal for the first time. Much of it is, however, a political analysis of Italy and even a polemical piece rather than sheer travel description. Already *The Lives of Haydn, Mozart and Metastasio*, and even more so his *History of Painting in Italy*, fuse historical surveys, esthetic judgments and sensitive readings of foreign mores. *A Roman Journal* and *Memoirs of a Tourist* are further examples of this peculiar blend of creative analysis. As for his novels, the evidence is clear. The tourist perspective is, so to speak, imposed on the reader in the very opening pages of the *Red and the Black;* the hypothetical Parisian traveler, through whose eyes we first glimpse the provincial town of Verrières and the surrounding landscape, sets the tone. The transient perspective establishes a feeling of mental mobility and ironic detachment. But it is also in the service of freedom. For social ties are confining.

As for the *Charterhouse of Parma*, it is in many ways a real travelogue. The arrival of Bonaparte's troops in Lombardy, the discovery of the joys of Milan, the beauty of Lake Como, Fabrice's escapade to Waterloo, life in and around Parma, the view from the Farnese tower, the crossing of the Po river—Stendhal has blended his own experiences of Italy, literary reminiscences, the adventures of a hero in search of his own authenticity and who, ironically, discovers, after sundry adventures, that true freedom is to be had within the confines of a jail. But then Stendhalian jails are something special; they are the perfect place for a reverie of space and movement.

The hedonistic nature of Stendhal's writings remains a permanent feature. But it is not a superficial titillation of the senses. True, this practitioner of the art of understatement prefers sensation to depth (or at least to the pretense of depth!); but the apparent frivolity, amateurism, dilettantism, and irrelevance must never fool the reader of Stendhal. That is why *Travels in the South of France* cannot be dismissed as a mere side-product. It is consonant with the major literary works of the author, and with an outlook on life.

*Victor Brombert*

Travels in the
South of France

What marvelous eyebrows these women of Angoulême have! They are indeed the "arches black as ebony" celebrated in *The Thousand and One Nights!*

Like Perugia in Italy, like Rieti, this town lies on top of a hill shaped like a sugar loaf. From the western end of a promenade lined with rather handsome trees, one looks down over a beautiful valley and then upward to pretty hills on the opposite side that form an amphitheater parallel, it seems to me, to the hill on which Angoulême stands.

Angoulême is one of those towns that did not move down into the plain even after the hapless citizens had ceased to live in fear of being sacked every ten years. In the Middle Ages the people of Angoulême were protected by the King of France. But the king was far away and they were under constant pressure from the hot-tempered lords of the surrounding country who fought each other on the slightest pretext, for well they knew that the citizens' money would save them from the annoyances of destitution brought on by squandering vast sums on wars.

Along the banks of the Charonte, just before we started to climb up to Angoulême, my eyes were charmed by the sight of the first buds on rows of elder trees that were beginning to show signs of life after the extremely harsh winter of 1837–1838.

3

*Angoulême*

# ·◦[ Bordeaux, *Sunday, March 11, 1838* ]◦·

Left Paris on March 8th at a quarter to five in the afternoon and arrived in Bordeaux on Sunday, March 11th, at four-fifteen in the morning. I was so drowsy from fatigue that I did not notice when we crossed the famous Bordeaux bridge to which I had been looking forward with such pleasure.

Toward half-past four the stagecoach drew up almost directly opposite the theater, on the magnificent quay called the Allées de Tourny. A street porter took charge of my possessions and I arrived at Monsieur Baron's, at the Hôtel de France, so completely exhausted that I was afraid I had left half of my luggage in the coach—a misfortune that happens to me quite frequently. I have a fairly good room, narrow and high-ceilinged, with one window, Number 21A. I slept until one o'clock in the afternoon and woke to find that it had rained. At two o'clock I went to the Café du Théâtre for lunch. The only newspaper was dated Thursday; as a matter of fact I had made the journey in seventy-one and three quarters hours. The mail coach takes only forty-three hours, I am told, but it left Paris on Friday, twenty-five hours after I did.

Supreme beauty of the magnificent quay of the Garonne, which I found even finer than I had remembered it. I have had many thoughts on revisiting Bordeaux, which I had seen briefly in 1828, but I am too tired to write them down. It is ten o'clock at night (still Sunday); I have just come from hearing *La Juive*. The leading role not badly sung by Madame Pouilly who, though lacking in beauty of person, possesses a beautiful voice, not at all shrill. I found a fairly good dinner and fairly good company at the hotel where I am staying. However, that dinner, which began at a quarter past five, was served in a vast, low-ceilinged room, on the ground floor, but so dark, without any light whatsoever, that there can not be a gloomier room even in Geneva! And yet here we are in Bordeaux, the center of Gascon vivacity, a city more southern in temperament than Valence.

5

When, toward midnight, on a beautiful moonlight night, you come out of the rue Saint-Catherine and see on your right that magnificent rue du Chapeau-Rouge, on your left the rue des Fossés de l'Intendance, and facing you the Place du Théâtre with, beyond it, the Place de Tourny and glimpses of the trees on the Quinconces, you wonder whether any city in all the world has such an imposing sight to offer. Note that the rue du Chapeau-Rouge, which ends at the bottom of the street in the masts of ships that cover the Garonne, rises toward the Place du Théâtre on a magnificent slope which the rue des Fossés de l'Intend-ance continues. That street ends in the large and symmetrical Place Dauphine.

From this point, the view of the Garonne and of the multitude of ships is blocked by the baths, an old, squat building, which should be pulled down and moved to the baths of the Quinconces.

In Bordeaux you are constantly being brought up short by the sight of a magnificent house. What could be more delightful than the view from the Café Montesquieu over the Quinconces? I would like to mention in particular a certain house on the rue des Fossés at the corner of a cross street, but the streets here seldom have names on them. The city fathers, who are very economical in this sort of expenditure, claim that everyone knows the streets, so why put up signs.

All the first floors of the houses in Bordeaux are beautiful, the majority being twelve or fifteen feet high with magnificent balconies four feet wide, facing the street. The cornices, toward the top of the houses, lack width, which makes them look small and gives a rather shabby effect. Their overly elaborate decorations are in extremely bad taste, and further shorten their dimensions, but should the eyes of Bordeaux citizens ever notice these defects, they could easily be rectified.

I visited the church of the Feuillants in the hope of seeing Mon-taigne's tomb, but the priest whose duty it is to unlock the chapel had carried off the key.

The thing that strikes the traveler from Paris most are the fine fea-tures of the women in Bordeaux and the beauty of their eyebrows. In Paris one too often sees heavy, common features that sometimes express

*Allée de Tourny*

very subtle thoughts. Here, however, subtlety is innate, and the faces unconsciously wear a proud, sensitive expression. As in Italy, here, too, the women have that fine air of gravity from which it would be so sweet to rouse them.

This thought struck me yesterday as I came out of vespers service around three o'clock; I was strolling on the handsome Place du Théâtre, which is called the Allées de Tourny, and had reached the street that leads to the Place du Chapelet just as *le beau monde* emerged from that fashionable church. Ideal beauty, *à la Schidone,* of the young girl selling oranges and bouquets of violets on the street corner: her charming coquetry, like a mere impulse of mingled vanity and friendliness toward a country bumpkin she knew, who walked past *without speaking to her.*

What adds to the charming effect of their natural delicacy of features is that, at least so far, I have not noticed the slightest affectation. No doubt there is some, but a man coming out of broad sunlight into a grotto finds it rather hard at first to see.

Yesterday I began my outings by walking the length of that admirable semicircle the Garonne makes in front of Bordeaux. I saw again the beautiful promenade that has replaced the Château-Trompette, demolished either in 1814 or 1815. Such is tradition that no one can give me the exact date.

The trees are quite young, but most of them are well on to thirty feet high and they form an arch. How different it would have been if they had planted chestnut trees instead of gloomy elms!

The hill opposite, on the right bank and two kilometers beyond the Garonne, is a delight to the eye. It ends at the river in the village of Lormont, on the northern extremity of that beautiful semicircle. The Garonne runs north. The town is on the left bank to the west and the Lormont hill occupies the right bank.

Bordeaux is unquestionably the most beautiful city in France. It slopes down toward the Garonne and from all sides there is a fine view of that lovely river so crowded with ships that it would be impossible to stretch a rope from one shore to the other without passing over one of them. As it was Sunday all the ships were beflagged.

After two hours spent in admiring them, I was obliged to leave that wonderful quai des Chartrons, that handsome promenade des Quin-

*La Grosse Cloche et les Fossés*

conces which has replaced the Château-Trompette. The bright March sun to which I had imprudently exposed myself had given me a headache. I hailed a cab.

"Rue des Minimes, Number 17."

That was the address of Montaigne's house. I found it had been torn down four years ago and a police barracks now stands in its place. Well now, gentlemen of Bordeaux, could you not spend even twenty-five francs to have the stonecutter engrave the following words on one of those square stone blocks in the barracks' wall that has replaced the houses from Number 10 to Number 23: "ON THIS SPOT STOOD MONTAIGNE'S HOUSE. IT WAS NUMBER 17 AND WAS TORN DOWN IN 1833."

I returned to the Feuillants to visit his tomb which I remembered well, particularly because of the absurd epitaph on it. The caretaker said to me: "Monsieur, have you spoken to Abbé N.?"

"I do not have the honor of knowing him."

"He's the one who has the key to the church. It's open only from eight to nine o'clock in the morning. Now if you knew Abbé N., you could arrange to meet him and visit Montaigne's tomb."

Poor Montaigne! Placed in the custody of one of those abbés who are trying to prevent the ladies of the Charity Society from giving a ball next Saturday in mid-Lent! This has been the first thing to offend me since I left Paris. It is not much, to tell the truth; moreover I do not offer my feelings as a model, far from it. I am merely writing down my impressions which frequently, it is true, can not withstand the full light of print.

Getting out of my cab I began to wander around the environs of the Cours d'Aquitaine (in Paris we would call it boulevard d'Aquitaine). I looked at the Gallo-Grecian façade of the hospital and the old Gothic church of Sainte-Eulalie opposite the barracks. From there I hurried back to the banks of the Garonne, going down the street toward the Arch of Triumph which stands at the end of the bridge.

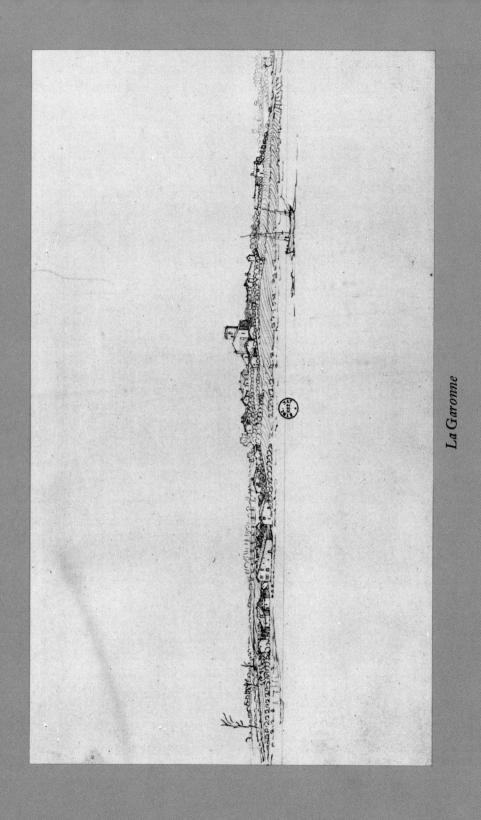

*La Garonne*

*Bordeaux: a View of the Port*

My critic could say: "Yes, Bordeaux is the most beautiful city in France because of the width of its streets, squares, boulevards, and quays, but not because of the style of its buildings."

I would reply: "Bordeaux has nothing, or almost nothing, as ugly as those hideous monuments that are the pride of Paris: the Grenelle fountain, the Saint-Gervais portal and others that Voltaire and his century were so fond of; but the houses in Bordeaux are much better than the houses built in Paris before 1837." (A year ago three or four houses that have a certain style were built on the boulevards; for example a house this side of the Porte Saint-Denis which copies fairly well the style of Palladio's imitators.)

The houses in Bordeaux are all Louis XV in style but ennobled by space. They are built of beautiful white stone which is not very hard; I watched the masons cutting it. The floors are not crowded close one upon the other; nor do the decorations around the windows and the cornices beneath the roof look as stereotyped as is usual in that abominable style. What a pity the architects who designed the Bordeaux buildings after the Château-Trompette was demolished in 1815 had not seen Rome or at least Genoa! Everything in this city is in that insipid Louis XV style imported by the Maréchal de Richelieu who ruled Bordeaux a long time with a rod of iron. Here all the first floors are handsome and high-ceilinged: see for example the magnificent rue du Chapeau-Rouge. Even south of that street, that is to say, in the oldest part of the town, the streets are broad and often crossed by fine boulevards. The houses on those ancient streets are, in general, no more than two stories high, sometimes only a single story, for almost all of these streets are on a slope, a situation which has many advantages.

I admire the inhabitants of Bordeaux and their completely epicurean way of life, a far cry from the crafty and ambitious hypocrisy of Paris. But, after all, truth cries out to me: "What kind of a writer is a man who lies?" It is therefore with real regret that I must admit: this theater of which the people of Bordeaux are so proud is architecturally of no value at all. Smooth Corinthian columns, thin and awkwardly placed, support an enormous entablature which is weighed down by twelve

13

*Bordeaux: the Theatre*

ridiculous statues. If you move back a pace you will notice an ugly roof, very large and heavy. On the whole, it is larger than, but perhaps just as ugly as the Odéon in Paris. This building, which stands alone between a square and three streets, is shockingly massive. On the three sides not filled by the twelve thin Corinthian columns, stand very heavy pilasters. Behind those enormous pilasters is a fairly dark passage-way which can be used as a covered walk and where, as a matter of fact, I walked for one hour this evening to keep out of the rain. But I was alone. This gloomy portico is no place for a rendezvous, like the portico in Brescia, for instance. The east side of the theater opposite the façade is not as ugly as the rest of the building.

This large, detached edifice ends in the middle of the square known as the Allées de Tourny and as, being slightly set back, it forms an angle with the axis of that square, a portico with a little style to it would make an excellent effect. But if an architect's monuments are to speak to the heart, the architect himself must have a heart. And there is nothing rarer in France. There people make fun of heart; look at old Corneille. The proud heart of a true architect is often displeasing to Power: witness the life of Michelangelo. Now, the architect can do nothing if he does not please the Minister. Architecture will therefore be the last of the arts to be revived in France.

Yesterday, Sunday, the day I arrived, I read a rather well-written article in a Bordeaux newspaper: "Our auditorium, the most beautiful in France and even in all Europe . . ." This flagrantly erroneous state-ment, offshoot of Gascon vanity, might nevertheless be extremely use-ful. *Noblesse oblige:* because the Bordelais believe the beauty of their theater to be supreme, they may imagine that they love the arts and will spend a little money to cultivate a sense of beauty in their children.

The interior of this theater where this evening I heard that mean-ingless music of *La Juive* (not too badly sung by Madame Pouilly), is very comfortable. The rather bare *atrio* (lobby) is decorated with col-umns that are much too thin, like those on the front of the building. On the first landing of the grand staircase at the back of this lobby, I found a ridiculous bust in the Louis XV style imprisoned behind a railing: it was a bust of Victor Louis, the architect immortalized by this hall which was built in 1773.

The interior of this properly so-called hall is perhaps the ugliest thing in this whole building. The section ordinarily given over to the spectators is usurped by eight enormous Corinthian columns that run the length of the semicircular wall and separate the loges which jut out into the auditorium like so many balconies rounded at the corners. I have never seen anything more hideous. It is not cheap and shabby like the barns that serve as theaters in a number of provincial towns, Grenoble for instance; it is ridiculous and makes you want to boo the architect. The ground-floor loges, which are even more absurd, were cut down to a decent shape several years ago when gods and goddesses were being painted on the ceiling.

There is no lack of stupid detail in this theater. From the orchestra stalls, for instance, you can not see the dancers' feet and yet in Bordeaux, the ballet is the thing they like best.

I thoroughly appreciated a good fire that was burning in a very dirty-looking panelled fireplace where the panelling had once been painted gray. Above it hung a portrait of Romainville, that excellent Crispino[1] who, in 1784, aroused transports of joy in Bordeaux.

[1] Crispino, valet, manservant of comedy. (Translator's note)

*Bordeaux: a View from la Bastide*

This morning, forgetting the cares of the world for two hours, I breathed in the first whiffs of soft spring air on that admirable quay, the center of which is distinguished by two rostral columns. Of this quay the Bordelais might truthfully say what they are constantly repeating about their theater: that it has not its equal in France and perhaps in all Europe, Naples excepted. And yet the quai de Bordeaux has a beauty that is wholly lacking in Chiaia—the sight of all that bustling activity and of the many ships that arrive daily from all parts of the world. It would take too long to count them, but to the eye of the beholder they seemed to be innumerable; and yet they were not drawn up, as they are in London, in that orderly fashion so necessary to commerce, but so inimical to any idea of beauty.

It was hard to tear myself away from that wonderful activity, that life on the quai de Bordeaux, to pursue the role of traveler and visit Saint André's.

Monsieur Millin was a typical academician, as servile as he was vain. His name on the title page of his journey is followed by fourteen lines in fine print enumerating all the academies to which he belonged. Of Saint André's, he says that . . .[2]

Styles have changed. Today Monsieur Millin would go into ecstacies, indulging in extravagant phrases copied from Monsieur de Chateaubriand, over the sublime beauty of Saint André's. In 1826, Monsieur Boutard, who held the scepter of fine arts on the *Debats*, said, . . . These blasphemies can no more detract from Saint André's than can the turgid phrases of modern praise with which unscrupulous persons seek to court society and, by gaining its esteem, obtain all the social advantages. What is left on buildings is, it seems to me, the expression of the emotion a sincere heart has felt in their presence.

This noble church of Saint André, built by the English in 1252, has only one very large nave, shaped like a playing card. The groined vault is marked by a number of strongly projecting ribs. One enters the church beneath a Renaissance portico and descends seven or eight steps

[2] Throughout his diary Stendhal leaves out dates, quotations, etc. which he probably intended to fill in later and replaces them with ellipses. (Translator's note)

*Bordeaux: the Port*

into the nave, an arrangement not at all incongruous with the very elegant Gothic form of this edifice.

To the right and left are three round columns, from which rise, without abacus or capital, the beginnings of the Gothic arch. Then come four groups of thin colonnettes forming half-columns. The partitions in this unique nave jut out into the transept on the right and on the left so as to form an acute angle.

The thickness of the wall of the nave is accentuated at the windows by the decorations on the two interior and exterior partitions which leave the space between them in shadow. Beyond the transept this single nave opens into three chapels separated by Gothic arches. The one in the middle is the choir; the two others surround it and meet at the Lady Chapel, at the most eastern point in the church. The chapels opening on the double aisles of the choir are well lighted.

I had entered Saint André's by the north portal. On the pillar that divides this portal in half is the stone statue of a pope, his hand raised in benediction: it is said to be Clement V. He is surrounded by three cardinals on the right and three on the left, whose faces remind one of naïve, young country priests. The draperies are poorly treated, but not so badly as the nude parts. This sculpture is by no means unsympathetic, but I missed the baldness and even the drama of present-day statuary which would have dispelled any suggestion of silliness. The north door is flanked by two high towers topped by lofty stone spires.

Leaving the church through the south door, I looked around for the façade: there was not a sign of it! After wandering around the adjacent streets, I went back to the Clement V door, and still searching for the façade, entered the church again and left it by the main door beneath the organ, opposite the choir. There I came upon a passageway and, as I turned around, I noticed a two-story building, its windows covered by pretty blinds: that was all there was to the façade of Saint André's! I laughed heartily at the anxiety with which I had been searching for this façade. As I circled the church I had passed this building and its door, which is perhaps seven feet wide, but it had never occurred to me to enter.

The pictures above the altars, which are set against the two walls of this single nave, are in particularly bad taste. They are far removed from the manual skill and bombastic emptiness of the school of 1837.

*Bordeaux: the Bridge and Railroad Station*

These pictures look as though they were the first efforts of some trades person. Though reminiscent of the innocence of a country church, they do not irritate as do silly and pretentious paintings.

Opposite the pulpit on the right is a fairly good copy of the *Martyrdom of Saint Peter* by Guido Reni (Vatican).

I read Archbishop Donnet's Lenten pastoral letter very carefully. It seemed to me far superior to the usual pastoral letter though he is always inveighing against *human reason*. The Archbishop, who is said to have a sense of humor, is quite right: our form of government constantly calls for self-examination and incites us to mistrust. What is going to become of religion in the midst of those two cruel enemies? In general, the Frenchman of our day is afraid of being taken for a dupe, despises everything, sees Robert Macaires[3] on all sides and believes in nothing. That is the sum total of all the talk I have overheard in the eight days I have been traveling. I have kept notes of all these remarks, particularly those I heard in Tours and at the table d'hôte in Angoulême.

To the east of Saint André's, there is a fine Gothic tower that stands alone, the tower of Peyberland which is also a belfry. I like Saint André's very much, but I must admit that it does not remind one of an inexorable hell like that dull commonplace cathedral of Tours which I find very ugly.

[3] Robert Macaire: a character in the *Auberge des Adrets* and a typical swashbuckling bandit. Daumier depicted him as a crooked businessman. (Translator's note)

How can I worthily describe my reception by my old friends from the colonies? A little more and my head would be turned. Lucky the traveler who can spend an evening with a family like the one I met yesterday! Not the slightest affectation about them. They treated me as though I were one of the sons of the house. Only, as I had come from Paris, they asked many questions about the way in which the Place de la Revolution was laid out. I described the gloomy rostral columns and the bridge built over the moat at the Tuileries. The ladies had not understood anything from the newspaper's description.

Society in Bordeaux is never sad and serious; at least I have not observed a single case of that frightful malady in the three houses to which I have so far been invited. I attended a charming society comedy, followed by a ball, not two paces from a distinguished personage who is ordinarily very stiff and reserved. No one could have a more pleasing and friendly countenance, no one could be more gracious or more disposed to meet all well-bred men and women on an equal footing. I regret that I can not mention the name of this person who is not nearly so haughty as any assistant office manager in Paris.

The Bordelais have little of that nonsense I would call "antechamber patriotism." Two delightful old gentlemen, worth millions, told me last evening: "You have seen our museum, sir. What a dull collection! We Bordelais have no appreciation of the arts. Three years ago I contributed money for a statue of Montaigne and for one of Montesquieu, which were to adorn the Allées de Tourny. The King deigned to contribute one hundred *écus*. Well, sir, there is no longer any question of those statues!

One of the finest painters in Paris, a man whose beautiful works we have admired, asked 5,000 francs to take the place of the drawing teacher in our school. The committee thought that was too expensive! No, my dear sir, we do not appreciate the fine arts. In Bordeaux we lead very material lives and, for that matter, get along better than anywhere else."

"Gentlemen," I told them, "you may lack an appreciation of the arts, but I find here an old French quality: frankness, and an absence of hypocrisy, for which perhaps I would look in vain in every other large city in France."

In spite of the rainy weather, I took a fiacre to the end of the city to see the Carthusian monastery of Saint Bruno and the cemetery. Bordeaux has no street as ugly as many streets in Rome and in Lyons. The streets in this English city are always wide enough. In the poorer quarters the houses are only one story high and as one approaches the outskirts of the city they have only a ground floor.

Saint Bruno: a great square hall, as long as a tennis court, and covered by an enormous roof. The façade is in the ridiculous Italian style that was fashionable around 1650, at a time when Italian architecture sank to the level of Monsieur Dupaty's letters on Italy.

Saint Bruno's has only one nave, lined twelve feet high with very elegant and highly polished wood paneling. The far end of this vast hall is faced with varicolored marble and filled with pillars, columns and bad sculpture. It is all petty, mean, striving for witty effects which you can guess in advance, absolutely in the Dupaty style. I was not surprised to find on the doors to the right and left the date 1672. Though the decorations are in bad taste, nevertheless they are better than in the church of Saint Nicholas-aux-Bains which my driver told me was built by the Duchess (the Duchess de Berry) and which is nothing but a barn with six pillars to the right and left surmounted by arches. The choir of Saint Bruno's has a rather pretty head of the angel making the Annunciation (on the left at the back of the choir), but the angel's body is pitiful. The base of the statue bears the coat of arms of a cardinal.

While I was in Saint Bruno's, suddenly a great darkness descended: the west wind blew in heavy gusts, rain beat violently against the windowpanes. This musical effect of wind and rain gave me more of a religious feeling than did the architecture of the church. I am writing this on the white marble balustrade that marks off the choir, which is lined with the same marble as the church where the architecture is only painted; however, this architecture is gay, light and pleasing to the eye, especially to a spectator from the North. What could be gloomier than the vast interior walls of Saint Sulpice or of Saint Roch? The architecture of Saint Bruno's in Bordeaux reminds one—but with less feeling of the grandiose—of the airy and charming architecture in the paintings of Paolo Veronese or of the beautiful streets of Genoa. Notice that had

*Bordeaux: the Tower and Cathedral of Saint André*

I come upon a church painted like this in Italy, words would have failed me to express my scorn. But here we are in an arid desert: even a tiny stream of brackish water delights us.

Fairly good picture of Saint Jerome on the right as one enters: then several fair to middling copies, grayish-yellow in color, of a few paintings by Le Sueur, still sublime in spite of that transformation. To my mind Le Sueur is decidedly the leading painter in France. Though his hand knew its craft, he also had something to say, whereas Poussin seems to me only a corollary of Raphael, with the strength of Polidoro da Caravaggio for example, plus a certain talent for landscape painting.

In a chapel to the left of the choir, there is a ridiculous epitaph on the tomb of Madame Béziade d'Avaray, 1691, wife of Monsieur de Sourdis, lieutenant general, who called himself "illustrious." The literature of the monarchy, mingled with ideas of chivalry, is incapable of producing a good epitaph. The sentiments they express, always mixed with the necessary drama, fall too far below real seriousness. Monarchy is always afraid that simplicity may appear middle class, which is why the monarchy, as an exception to the rule of clarity, uses Latin for epitaphs. The epitaph of Madame de Sourdis, who died very young, is in French. Pitiful sculpture on that tomb: bad bust of the *illustrious* Monsieur de Sourdis and his young wife.

In the chapel on the left, as one enters, an excellent or at least a very good bust of Cardinal de Sourdis, but it is placed too high; fair bust of that good Monsieur de Cheverus whom Bordeaux has recently lost. Because of the charity ball, which was to have taken place on March 22nd in mid-Lent, and for which 5,000 francs had already been collected, his death was keenly regretted. All Bordeaux society was talking about that ball.

Next to Saint Bruno's lies Bordeaux's magnificent cemetery. I don't know why this cemetery reminds me of the one in Bologna. This one has no monuments, but it does have magnificent plane trees, forty to fifty feet high. A pity the city fathers of Bordeaux, faithful to the imbecility that title implies, had not planted plane trees on the Quinconces instead of gloomy elms! What a touch of genius it would have been to plant the Quinconces with chestnut trees! They would be in bloom today, March 19th!

On each grave there is a little garden about eighteen inches high by five feet long and one foot wide. I counted eleven carnation plants and one pansy plant, the latter in bloom, on the tomb in front of which I am writing.

On the humble grave, next to the monument of the Marshallin Moreau, all the flowers are in full bloom and the air around is redolent with their perfume.

Pretty, very pretty little Greek temple with four columns erected by Monsieur Marmiché to conjugal love. Unfortunately the sculpture that goes with this temple is execrable, especially the nude forms. There is perhaps nothing in Père La Chaise in as good taste as this little temple.

For the first time this year I have seen the green of the willows in full leaf. Inscriptions in the Bordeaux necropolis are infinitely less ridiculous than those in Père La Chaise. This is because of the formula generally used: "Tomb or burial place of such and such a family." I noticed the tomb of a Monsieur de Haumont, born in Martinique, February 31 (*sic*), 1795. Many Spanish graves. Many other graves decorated with the image of a brave soldier of the Italian army of 1796. This morning the meadow to the left of this city of the dead was inundated, showing the effect of the abominable rains that are tormenting us this year. Above the rise of ground beyond that inundated field, I could see in reverse all the towers of Bordeaux, the two church steeples, the steeple of Saint André, the tower of Saint Michel, etc. . . .

This afternoon I went to Saint Seurin's, it was closed. At every turn in Bordeaux, one comes upon paths lined with trees thirty to forty feet high. Unfortunately they are always gloomy elms.

This evening, charming picnic dinner at the Café de Paris. These pleasant Bordelais lead a wholly physical, carefree, out-of-doors life, admirable at a time when hypocrisy is polluting the moral life of France.

One of the diners, a winebroker, was being teased about the good life he led. The only capital these gentlemen put in their business is a horse and a tilbury in which they run all over Médoc, a land that produces good wine, from Bordeaux to the Tour de Cordouan on the left bank of the Gironde. They taste the wines of the various proprietors and, with a piece of chalk, mark the quality on the casks. You can imagine how the proprietors pay court to them! And woe betide the owner who would dare to rub out the broker's chalk mark! No broker would take it upon himself to sell that man's wine.

After he has received his mail, a merchant will say to a broker: "I need 200 casks of wine, of such and such a quality, at such and such a price."

The winebroker replies: "There are some in this place and that place." He then goes to the proprietors and charges 2 per cent above the price paid by the merchant, in addition to gifts from the proprietors who are always eager to sell. These brokers are like ministers: they always call on people who need them. Many of them make 8–10,000 francs a year from their travels around Médoc and by allowing themselves to be urged to accept good dinners. Besides they can never lose.

My neighbor, a merchant who had first tried to teach me about the wines of Médoc and was now, I thought, trying to impress me, swore that there were as many clubs in Bordeaux as there are in Geneva. I was told there were even clubs for servants: a club for servants who were not coachmen, and a club for coachmen. The poor wives never go to the theater because their husbands don't like to take them. On the other hand, Bordeaux is perhaps more plagued than any small town by the fear of "what will people say." If a young man calls at a house three times, the lady (moaning) begs him not to come so often.

This sort of life gives birth to passion. By an accident, very strange surely in 1838, there is such a thing as *love* in Bordeaux. The presence of this rare flower is proved by elopements as senseless as possible and which, while they ruin the lover, do not even give him the satisfaction of conceit, for his life will be lost in the vortex of Paris.

Today, third rainy day; at four o'clock I shall go to see Saint Seurin's.[4]

On the plateau, to which one climbs by way of the handsome rue du Chapeau-Rouge, beyond a square planted with trees, rises the church of Saint Seurin. One enters by the north door at the far end of the right transept. This door leads into an *atrio* or hexagonal vestibule making it easy for the faithful to go in and out when it rains. Five sides of the vestibule are extremely plain; the sixth, formed by one side of the church is, on the contrary, very ornate and has thirteen almost life-sized statues. They are apparently from the Middle Ages and of no

[4] In my opinion, a Romanesque church repaired twenty years ago. Will that prove to be true?

value. One or two even have those enormous, disproportionate heads that remind the citizen of Paris of the statues at the north gate of Saint Denis'. The draperies on those statues are fairly good; it is the nude parts that are ridiculous.

The façade of the church has no ogival arch but many semicircular arches; it is embellished by two very insignificant statues of bishops in the mediocre style of the XVII century. Above the door is another bas-relief, even worse perhaps, which forms a pyramid in accordance with all the academic rules. Except for the sculpture, this façade would not be bad if it had the color of antiquity like Saint Croix', for example. It leads to an *atrio* painted white, but which is in fact worthy of respect because of its age. To the left and right attached columns in a group of Gothic columns have three-storied capitals, all three of them boldly projecting, which tells us the year. . . .

The interior of the church is very plain. The groins in the vault are marked by heavy ribs like all those I have seen in Bordeaux. The vault is supported by two enormous round pillars on the right and two pillars on the left. These pillars are not far from the outside wall to which they are attached by a semicircular arch. On each side of the pillars is a Gothic group of ribbed piers.

The tomb of Saint Seurin is under the high altar and his story is carved in the fourteen compositions on the reredos that decorate it. Under the choir is a crypt where the relics of Saint Feure[5] are worshipped.

[5] Saint Fort: first bishop of Bordeaux. (Translator's note)

Still raining. Fourth day of rain. This morning, at eight o'clock in Bordeaux, I boarded the steamboat for Blaye. Drops of rain fell every quarter of an hour and every two hours there was a downpour. This was all caused by the west wind.

I learned that we were to arrive in Blaye at noon.

"Don't you go any farther?" I asked the clerk who collected the fares.

"We go to Pauillac."

"Well then, a ticket to Pauillac."

"You should have taken the boat from Royan," this polite clerk volunteered. "It goes ten miles farther than we do."

In spite of the rain I remained on deck. I wanted to have a good look at that admirable Lormont hill which is a series of rounded hillocks, their summits crowned by country villas and huge trees. After the village of Lormont, this chain of hills turns away from the Garonne and runs toward the Dordogne. Those hills are said to be covered with charming country houses. I could see one chateau of bright red brick in the Fontainebleau style.

I noticed, also on the left bank of the Garonne, the swampy chateau in which Monsieur de Peyronnet[6] lives. There, so a sailor told me, he makes two hundred barrels of good, very full-bodied marsh wine. This wine is very much sought after for shipping to Mauritius; the sea is good for it and the owner sells it for 200 francs a barrel, aged two or three years.

I saw the Bec d'Ambès, a meadow that lies between the Dordogne and the Garonne. As everyone knows, the magnificent river, formed by these streams after they leave Bec d'Ambès, is called the Gironde. We steamed past the la Roque quarries which produce that fine soft white stone that makes Bordeaux so beautiful. I saw Blaye and its citadel which formerly belonged to the Duc de Saint-Simon, father of the great historian. What a contrast between the way people talk politics in Bordeaux and the way they talk politics in Nantes! They talk about the

[6] Count Charles-Ignace de Peyronnet (1778–1854): French statesman born in Bordeaux. He was Minister of the Interior in 1830. (Translator's note)

*On the Road*

capture of Blaye the way one would talk of a battle waged under King Jean. The common sense of the Bordelais is admirable; nothing disturbs him; he never plays a part; he is interested only in those conditions that make it possible for him to lead a good life.

Suddenly we noticed on the left bank of the river eight or ten handsome three-storied houses rather like rich country estates: this was Pauillac. None of those dirty, crowded buildings near the river, the business center in old towns! Could Pauillac be entirely new? One would say that three-quarters of the town was not thirty years old. I engaged a room in Monsieur Delhomme's hotel on the quay.

Lighting my cigar, I went out at one o'clock at a loss as to how I could pass the time until ten o'clock tomorrow. As I was climbing a hilly street, I saw a stagecoach that was making ready to leave; they had just shut the door.

"Where is it going?"

"To Lesparre."

"And once in Lesparre would I find a way to get back here this evening?"

"The mail coach leaves there at seven and gets here at ten."

I climbed aboard the stagecoach. This was one of those days in which to recall ordinary events is real drudgery. How different from my journey to Italy! I am therefore writing in the coach as we go along.

Gently undulating terrain which, on the whole, forms a plain, but where you would seldom find five hundred feet of level ground. From a distance, the land appears to be bare. Vines cover everything that is not pine woods. They stretch out in long straight rows of vine arbors, scarcely a foot above the ground which, in turn, is divided into an endless number of little elevations shaped like a capital A, the highest point being covered by lines of vine stocks.

The arbor is supported by vertical stakes eighteen inches long, six inches of which are hidden in the ground. Young pines, no thicker than a thumb, are used for the horizontal line. They are sown as thick as hemp and half of them are pulled up when they become ten or twelve feet high.

First I found, in this rather deserted land, several large trees surrounding a sort of chateau with a tower. A little later I came to a

strange building which had only a ground floor. "Those are stables belonging to a rich landowner whose chateau is a quarter of a mile from
the road," the postilion told me. I thought that it was more probably a
*chai*: that is what the people in this region call a wine cellar or a wine
factory! This very elegant building, brilliant light yellow in color was
not, to tell the truth, in any particular style, neither Greek nor Gothic;
but it was very gay and rather in the Chinese style. On the façade you
could read the single word: *Cos.* Among the vineyards were round
crenelated towers; shelters for the vine grower's tools and for himself
during a storm. These towers, which I have already seen in the neighborhood of Blaye, are a very pretty sight.

The undulating plain went on and on. Then we came to great pine
forests, not very high but mixed with clumps of oak trees and cuttings
of underbrush. Very few houses or men in this flat countryside. I look
admiringly at everything that is not woods and vineyards in this great
name of Médoc.

At last we came to a street of rather pretty houses: this was Lesparre. In memoirs from the days of Henri III, I think, there was a Duc
de Lesparre. This village, which the government has just made a sub-
prefecture district, has 1,300 inhabitants.

The street was so badly paved, though made of large stones as in
Paris, that the coach suddenly turned off and, not slackening speed but
still at a gallop, dashed along a road through the countryside around
the village. A few hundred paces farther on, after a second right-hand
turn, we entered the village, but now only at a trot for here there was
no public for the postilion to impress.

When I arrived at the Lion-d'Or, an admirably clean, English country inn kept by Monsieur Delhomme, I was dying of hunger. The host,
who looked very gloomy, told me I would find something to eat in his
house and he called Augustine, his wife, who looked quite nice but
seemed to be just as gloomy as her husband. This was a sample of the
"gentlemanly" manner instead of the straightforward frankness I had
expected to find in a country inn. As a matter of fact I was in a sub-
prefect inn. Moreover this was the only sign of affectation I had seen
since I came to Guyenne.

"What can you give me for dinner, Madame? I am terribly
hungry."

"We'll give you a bit of preserve, sir."

At the word, I shuddered.

"Monsieur," said my hostess, "it is preserve of duck."

"And when will it be ready?"

"In half an hour."

I took a walk around this town of 1,300 inhabitants. There were a number of well-stocked shops, among others, three clockmakers with clocks like those in Paris. These shops supply all the householders in Médoc. I saw two or three new houses, all of them built of handsome white stone, as pretty as the houses in Bordeaux, by which I mean prettier than those in Paris.

In a church whose bell tower and choir are Gothic with handsome ribs like those in Saint André's in Bordeaux, they have built a Greek nave. To judge by the apse surrounded on the outside by semicircular arcades, I would even think that the rear of this church was Romanesque. The Greek part, built a year or two ago, is vast and commodious.

I can only commend the Paris board of directors for government buildings for the law courts and prison they have built in Lesparre. All these buildings have been set at the back of a garden three hundred feet from the main street, a horribly ugly street whose ground was very expensive. This sign of common sense greatly shocked the people of the neighborhood. But nothing could be less expensive, nothing prettier than this little Greek temple, which one reaches by eight or ten steps, with its two main buildings set forward, the office of the clerk of the court, and the. . . . On the left is a charming prison (at least seen from the outside).

I saw an old and solidly built tower. "That was part of the Duc de Gramont's chateau," an old peasant told me. "It was pulled down." Those houses still belong to Monsieur de Gramont (apparently he is the aged nobleman I used to see at Monsieur de T.'s).

As I passed the clock shops I looked in to see whether the half hour would soon be up. How exquisitely clean my supper was! It consisted solely of a preserved thigh of duck and a handful of potatoes. And I had asked for a lot!

It rained for hours; then came a clearing. This weather is caused by that cursed west wind that pours all the waters in the ocean down upon us. Taking advantage of the brief clearing, I walked through the village again. There was coffee to be had, but no milk.

As it started to rain again, I took refuge in the inn's kitchen, where I admired its exquisite cleanliness. Though my hosts had prepared dinners for four or five arrivals in succession, I have never seen anything as clean. It was such a pleasure to watch them at their work that I almost wanted to have dinner all over again. Face and expression more than half-Spanish of the mistress of the house, a woman of thirty, very serious and taciturn.

Two very polite old women servants, a politeness more subtle even than in Paris. They asked me indirect questions in an effort to discover who the devil had managed to persuade me to visit Lesparre. I bought a copybook in which to write this estimable diary. This copybook, which I left rolled up in the dining room, caused much wonderment and perhaps will be worth a thought on the part of Monsieur the subprefect. As I was about to leave, the host, looking very important, said to me: "Monsieur, don't forget your papers."

At quarter past seven, an uncomfortable carriage whirled me like the wind to Pauillac, so fast that I pitied the horses.

At half-past nine I was told: "Why don't you go all the way to Bordeaux, Monsieur? Besides here you are in Pauillac."

I got out; it was raining and there I was apparently in the suburbs of Pauillac, in utter darkness. A gust of wind turned my umbrella inside out; no one on the road; all the houses shut tight.

I could not make out in which direction the Gironde lay. At last I remembered that this morning as I came ashore I had noticed a pretty octagonal bell tower, and I began looking everywhere along the roofs for my bell tower, but in that impenetrable darkness the roofs melted into the sky.

At last, slipping and stumbling over a wretched pavement full of holes filled with water, I came to the church, but I still could not discover in which direction the river flowed to the Gironde. Seeing an open shop, I asked very politely to be shown the way. At that moment it began to rain again.

Without a word a child of ten came forward, and going out ahead of me, said: "Come on." He led me on what seemed to me a very long detour which brought me at last to the hotel on the Parc. I entered and the child ran off. I was obliged to send someone after him to give him a little token of my generosity. Without him, I would have wandered around those confounded streets perhaps for hours.

It takes the genius of a great logician, something very rare in France, to guide a stranger who does not know a city. There is nothing more difficult: people always show the stranger the way by mentioning streets he has never heard of. The native should forget his own habits and put himself in the stranger's place. Even in the tiniest village I always guide myself by the polar star, like a great astronomer, but this evening how could I find the east where the Gironde flows? The sky was clad in somber black.

The mistress of the house and her two daughters welcomed me. They were seated in front of the fireplace working by the light of a candle secured to the mantelpiece by seven or eight little pieces of plated metal, which permitted each of the ladies to bring her light nearer. For they were really ladies and I was in good society in a pleasant room, seated in front of a blazing fire. How my lot had changed in five minutes!

Though I made the greatest effort to be charming, I met with little success. The young ladies remained silent, impassive. Perhaps that was good form in Pauillac. So, seeing this, I excused myself to go to bed and the ladies summoned the manservant. Admirable bedroom with four windows overlooking the river, which I had engaged on my arrival. Excellent bed and all that, with two delicious cups of coffee with milk —cost, 3 francs.

# ·◦[ Pauillac, *March 22* ]◦·

Beautiful sunshine at nine o'clock which impelled me to take a walk around the town. At ten o'clock, a terrific downpour, but fortunately I had just boarded the steamboat.

Pauillac is pleasantly situated: fine houses; the streets are hilly, but the paving execrable.

As for the church, surmounted by that pretty octagon-shaped bell tower, it is a fine new barn divided into three very irregular naves by eight beautiful Doric columns with pedestals fluted up to a height of eighteen inches. Nothing could be more suitable, nothing brighter but also nothing in the world less religious; aside from the cost, it is exactly like Notre-Dame-de-Lorette, a perfect symbol of the religious spirit in the France of 1838. The chapels are decorated with painted and gilded bas-reliefs on wood. Atrocious faces on those bas-reliefs. Pretty little ship hanging in the center of that very bright nave. I admired again the charming bell tower, but how different it is from the bell towers of country churches in Lombardy, not to mention those built by that excellent and very superior architect, the late Marquis Cagnole!

With 3,000 francs more, and the style of Palladio, they could give this chapel in Pauillac more character. But did anyone in the Department ever feel the religious spirit of a church?

A few trees have been planted on the Pauillac quay, but they are not plane trees. Most of the little street urchins who play on that river bank speak French. Sign above a door: Life and Fire Insurance.

On the steamboat, I stayed on deck in spite of the rain to admire the eight or ten handsome houses on the bank surrounded by trees that mean Pauillac to anyone arriving by the Gironde.

Now back on the boat again, exhausted from the wild gusts of a tremendous rainstorm, I appreciated the truth of Monsieur Gagnon's remark: "Reading helps one to exchange moments of boredom in life for pleasant moments." The only book I had with me was about a dull courtier and yet the boat passed Blaye without my noticing it. (The joy of having one's passion as a profession. Dominique's[7] situation.)

At last the glorious Lormont hillside came into sight again, that suc-

[7] Dominique: one of Stendhal's many pseudonyms. (Translator's note)

37

*Pauillac: Seen from the Lesparre Road*

cession of rounded hillocks crowned by factories and great trees.

In the evening, tea at Madame Mathé's. Monsieur has been on the point of buying Montaigne's estate where that famous author was born. The bedroom is still decorated with the frescoes his eyes gazed upon. The estate comprises eight farms; today it would be worth . . . , unfortunately the woods have been cut down. Montaigne's grandfather is known to have bought the property for ten thousand francs.

In the evening a masked ball; we danced in the auditorium and in a charming concert hall. I was shown into a handsome *loge*. The Lenten season and the fear of "what-will-people-say," the cruel malady that torments all Bordeaux, made it impossible for any woman of good standing to attend this ball. The misfortune that happened to the C.'s! I was so overcome with fatigue that this calamity touched me deeply and I went to bed at two o'clock in very low spirits.

| | |
|---|---|
| 1. Coupé on the stagecoach from Pauillac to Lesparre | 3 francs |
| Dinner at Lesparre, wine excellent | 2.50 |
| Price of return trip | 3. |
| Room and coffee at Pauillac | 3. |
| | 11.50 |
| Steamboat there | 3.50 |
| Back | 3.50 |
| | 7 |
| Total | 18.50 |

Third day of rain from the west wind. At the club they told me this weather could last for two weeks. I took a very elegant fiacre and visited the churches; there are not very many in Bordeaux.

Of them all, Saint Croix's is by far the strangest. I have just spent two hours there and I have a terrific headache from trying to see and judge the alleged "indecencies" of which a pretty woman spoke to me last evening, though to be sure in very decorous terms.

Saint Croix's seems to me to be a Romanesque church which was rebuilt under the influence of the Gothic; but the façade is Romanesque and a great many columns, so close together they almost touch, had been massed there before columns went out of style.

Saint Croix's very odd and, in my opinion, impressive façade is almost triangular in shape, very high on the right side and very low on the left. To the right of the spectator rises a three-storied tower. Each story has three windows, which end in a semicircular arch supported by two tall columns. On each floor, between the columns supporting the arches and the angle, are four imitation Corinthian columns almost touching each other.

On the left of this tower with its columns, is the façade of the church itself, a façade not lacking in elegance though the columns on the tower project over it. This façade is three stories high and today is a mass of wallflowers in full bloom. They cover the whole building which shows signs of neglect. It is incredible that the priest does not have the wallflowers torn down, though at midday, their freshness and their graceful shapes make a charming effect. Each year these flowers renew their youth side by side with the ruinous decay of that work of man, an architecture that dates back as far perhaps as the year 1100. On the ground floor of the façade are the main door of the church and two other doors that have been sealed off.

On the first floor there is a fine and comparatively modern rose window surrounded by seven semicircular arches; in addition, on the left, a large arch, slightly Gothic in style, and finally on the third floor an aperture closed by a pediment. On the left in the lowest part of the façade is a door with a hint of the characteristic Gothic point, and three semicircular windows set one above the other. This is a church full of unction, if one may call it that. Its antiquity, its air of being half destroyed by time, touches the visitor's heart.

Some portions of the façade, the little arcades, for example, seem to belong to the old Gothic period; on the other hand, the many, almost regular, columns that adorn the right tower, the only one that is high, would indicate the early Renaissance period. On each side of the main door I noticed short columns with flutings and zigzag decorations. You go down six steps to reach the floor of the church. There are three naves; attached Corinthian columns in the six pilasters that separate the naves. The paintings are not too bad. The archangel Michael stabs the devil; you can see the latter's fiery breath! Opposite is a Saint Francis, a copy of a painting from the school of Bologna. Rostrum of polished walnut with strange inserts in colored marble, as in Saint André's, Louis XV in style but not so displeasing as other things in that style.

The painted architecture ornamenting the back of the choir and the choir vaulting is very effective. Fairly good votive offering at the rear . . . wreathed columns . . . chapel of S . . . I read . . . the Iberian race . . . twelve years old who were present at the catechism. . . .

As I went out this morning at ten o'clock, I met six men and a child walking in the middle of the road. They looked very serious; their feet were bare, their heads uncovered, and they were mumbling solemn prayers. I thought they were part of a funeral cortege and to ward off the evil omen, I hastened to retrace my steps. But not seeing a coffin, I asked a woman who was calmly spinning on her doorstep what it was all about.

"They're sailors who've made a vow," she told me with great composure. So then I followed the procession, to which workmen busy at the doors of their shops paid little attention, as far as the church of Saint Dominique. There I learned that these men were sailors from the brig *Elisa* that had almost foundered in the last great storm. Seeing themselves in extreme danger, the sailors had made a vow and were saved.

Saint Dominique's, also called Notre Dame, is only two steps from the magnificent square known as the Allées de Tourny.

I do not know a more beautiful square in France. The trees have been removed because there are so many on the adjacent promenade of the Château-Trompette. This square leads into a garden through beautiful streets not fifty yards long and this is what gives the square its unique character. The houses on the west, apparently built in Monsieur de Tourny's lifetime, are only two stories high, with now and then a handsome second story surmounted by a little attic. The houses on the east, built apparently after Château-Trompette was demolished, are three and four stories high. They are magnificent and far superior to the houses Paris is putting up every day and in which architecture is barbarously sacrificed to wages.

A very ingenious and extremely practical portico closes this handsome square on the north. On the south it is terminated by the façade of the theater which appears in perspective, thus partially concealing the curious weight of that building and the painful thinness of the columns on the façade.

To tell the truth, I would be at a loss to suggest any additions to this square. Perhaps two pedestrian statues placed at each end; equestrian statues might dwarf the houses on the west. Michelangelo's *The Thinker* molded in bronze would go very well here.

There could be nothing more banal than the statue of that excellent administrator, Monsieur de Tourny,[8] who governed la Guyenne from 1743 to 1757, as an extremely well-made inscription informs us. He did for Bordeaux what, at the same period, no one ever thought of doing for Paris, as witness the ugliness of the Montmartre and Poissonière districts and everything north of the boulevards. When Monsieur de Tourny conceived the idea of beautifying Bordeaux and had the strength of character to carry it out, that sort of thing had not become commonplace in government circles; it took an inventive mind, a genius to assume such a task. Monsieur de Tourny is much anterior to Turgot who was minister in 1774 and whose work preceded by nine years the work of Adam Smith.

Monsieur de Tourny's successors, however, have certainly not followed in his footsteps. They have not even been distinguished save perhaps by the ridiculous names they gave to all the streets and roads that replaced the Château-Trompette. So far I have looked in vain for names of those immortal Girondins who, though they were undoubtedly wrong, nevertheless won everlasting fame. Perhaps there are still envious people in Bordeaux, like Barnave in Grenoble. The day those vulgar creatures cease to have a voice in the matter, Bordeaux will honor Vergniaud.[9]

There is another man who helped to demolish the Château-Trompette, and made Bordeaux, already admirably prepared by Monsieur de Tourny, the most beautiful city in France. This man, less fortunate than Louis XVIII, or the Prince de Condé, did not give his name to any street; he was Napoleon Bonaparte. Was it not Duclos[10] who said that the public as a whole, especially when ruled by city magistrates, responds only to commonplace ideas?

Most admirable of everything in Bordeaux are the foreheads and

[8] Marquis de Tourny, Louis (1690–1760): benefactor of the Limousin and la Guyenne. He did much to beautify Bordeaux. (Translator's note)
[9] Here are the names. (The author failed to supply them.)
  Pierre-Victurnien Vergniaud (1753–1793): member of the French National Convention. Born in Limoges, he was arrested with the Girondins and died on the scaffold. (Translator's note)
[10] Charles Pinot Duclos (1704–1772): author of *Considerations sur les moeurs* and member of the French Academy. (Translator's note)

eyebrows of the women and their charming vivacity expressed in innumerable gestures. Do not imagine that this vivacity bursts forth in extravagant gestures on the street as is the way in Naples. No, here there is more grace of movement. No depression, no gloom here: from the man loading his cart to the young girl selling violets on the street corner every movement is quick and lithe. Almost never is there any notion of force, almost always the sense of tact. The young girls selling flowers never wear that air of professional brashness which so disgusts one in Paris. You feel that her companions would scorn the young girl on the Paris boulevard if her glance, her tone of voice and her gestures did not defy modesty.

I suspect there is even *love* in Bordeaux and love promptly teaches the full value of modesty. In the four days (from March 11th) I have been here, I have not yet seen any brazen acts. None of those hideous women who hawk fish on the streets of Paris! Here the daughters of the common people cover their heads with a handkerchief. Their faces obviously reveal a mixture of the Iberian and the Gallic races. There are a few long faces, but more particularly, it seems to me, among the affluent classes, denoting a mixture of the Iberian and the Cimbrian races. Perhaps these quaint words will make the reader laugh; the thing exists, however, I am sure of it. In the boldness of the nose, in general not too large, the smooth beauty of the forehead, the admirably drawn eyebrows, one can recognize the Iberian race at twenty paces.

Never have I seen those faces heavy with flesh that are all too common in Paris, never any of those broad cheekbones separated by a flat nose. Throughout this whole day I have seen only one enormously fat face like the many faces one sees in Paris. The Iberian race, in general, has a thin face, I am trying to think of a well-known person such as Cardinal de Richelieu (see the admirable bust of the Cardinal on the ground floor of the Louvre, almost under the clock).

This evening, at the theater, the women of the leisure class, seated near me with their husbands on their right on the same bench and, apparently, their lovers on the benches behind them, laughed like young girls of eighteen. This would have sounded very strange in Paris. Here I was the only one among their neighbors to notice that laughter; and I gave thanks for the four or five degrees of latitude that separate the little theater in Bordeaux from the Gymnase in Paris. After that, need I mention the *simplicity*, the *naturalness*, the *lack of affectation* which strikes one in the manners of these people?

I have not yet presented any of my letters of introduction and if it were not that I feared I would be remorseful, I would really like to leave without presenting them. But then would I have the audacity to write about Bordeaux? Perhaps there is something very strange happening to society in these parts of which I am not aware.

Every afternoon, at five o'clock, I take the omnibus to a point opposite Lormont, this is to say, I circumnavigate the admirable semicircle that runs from the Saint Michel tower to the Bacalan quay and I look at all the merchant ships that have anchored in the Garonne, a hundred paces from the quay my omnibus passes. That quay is bustling with custom officers and sentries. What opportunities for smuggling there are in this port which is one hundred miles long on both shores! The customhouse collects . . . francs a month.

Two things make me think well of the Bordeaux municipal government:

1. It has none of that stupid language the Paris police write on walls: "Under penalty of punishment it is forbidden to . . ."

The Bordeaux municipality writes:

"By order and for the sake of health, it is forbidden to . . ." The authorities deign to reason with the citizens. At the moment it is no longer good form to make fun of their orders; everyone understands the sacred word "health."

2. This town council, appointed for life, models itself on the police of ancient Rome. Small buildings—I don't know whether there are as many as 154 as was the case in ancient Rome—and numbered water barrels make for great cleanliness. All minor infractions of the law, my driver told me, are punished by confiscating a man's hat, which he must then redeem from the policeman for several sous.

The cabs are extremely clean, much better kept than in Paris. The horses are thin, but their harness is well oiled. The coachmen are very polite. They could serve as models of Bordelais faces: they look smart, quick, alert, never thick-headed and coarse, drowned in flesh. In Bordeaux the men are appreciably shorter than in Paris. So far I have not met any young men who are caricatures of fashion like those I saw in Nantes, for instance, in July, 1837. There are not many red ribbons,[11] far fewer than in the cities of the North. Perhaps the crosses bestowed hit or miss to disparage the Order in 1815 have given out and have not been replaced.

I have seen only one thing to compare with the admirable drive from the tower of Saint Michel at Bacalan and that is the promenade on the *riva de' Schiavoni* in Venice. Here there is no façade with the distinctive genius of Palladio and his pupils, but a multitude of merchant vessels. One must also admit that the Lido of Venice can not stand comparison with the admirable hill, covered with great trees and handsome factories, which slopes down to the Garonne on jagged cliffs above the village of Lormont.

[11] Decoration of the Legion of Honor. (Translator's note)

# ⋅⋅◦] Bordeaux, *the . . .* [◦⋅⋅

Glorious sunshine. The leaves of almost all the trees on the Quinconces are massed against the sky. I was delighted to come upon the esplanade of the *grand café* in the shadow of the theater and to smoke a cigar there. On entering the café for a cup of chicory, I learned from the newspaper, *Mémorial Bordelais,* that the weather is freezing, that everyone is wearing heavy overcoats and that there is still no sign of spring to gladden nature. Are these the usual lies of a government newspaper or merely a desire to use ready-made phrases?

I looked at a thermometer in the shade at the end of the line of houses that have replaced the Château-Trompette—it registered 52 degrees F. Here there are at least twelve or fifteen really fine houses, much more imposing than any houses in Paris. There were several corbels, several ornaments with garlands of flowers; it is the ridiculous Louis XV style of architecture. The Capitole in Toulouse is even crowned by a double-bass.

Paris has nothing comparable to this row of houses overlooking an immense garden, with, on the right, a view of the Garonne crowded with ships and beyond it the hill of Lormont. I was told that those ships that were flying flags at the top of their masts were about to sail. The French ships are near the bridge which has brought in much retail business and has made those handsome houses modeled on houses on the Place Vendôme, unfashionable. Foreign ships cast anchor opposite les Chartrons which is why most wealthy Bordeaux merchants live on this magnificent quay or on the superb rue Pavée des Chartrons.

Most of the streets in Bordeaux have ridiculous names given with intent to flatter. Beginning with the year 1850, a circular from the Minister of the Interior should prohibit naming streets and squares after living men. The result would be that the present ministers would be the last great men to receive this sort of honor. No rue Vergniaud; no rue Valazé. The only street well named is the one on which my hotel stands: rue Esprit des Lois.

In this glorious sunshine there is nothing comparable to the Place Tourny which opens on the Quinconces. The houses on the west side, which date from the era of that excellent administrator, Monsieur de

Tourny (1743–1757), are only two stories high and are embellished with sculptured garlands of flowers. The houses on the east side, built since 1817, are very handsome and would be worthy of Italy, if the cornices of the roofs projected farther and if there were less carving on the balustrades, the covers over the windows and the poor little corbels supporting the roof. There is nothing virile in all this architecture; one longs for the somber gravity of a street in Arezzo. What effect would the gay magnificence of the palace of the post office in Venice have here? (I forget the name of the illustrious house that sold it.)

A Bordelais, a man with a sense of humor, who sold me some wine yesterday, found much fault with the two rostral columns east of the Quinconces which are actually the only pretty and well placed decorations in Bordeaux. But they have not yet been praised in a newspaper article from Paris!

On the Quinconces I would erect a bronze copy of Michelangelo's *The Thinker* and give him the features of the Black Prince whom Bordeaux loved so well at the end of the Middle Ages. Put up a statue to an Englishman, you say! That would be enough to make the English lower classes, who still hate us, die of rage. The people of Bordeaux should have their taste roused by the same fury Michelangelo felt. I have actually heard good society in this city admire the "graceful" figures in lithographs!

## Palais Gallien in the Faubourg Saint-Seurin

The Palais Gallien is an amphitheater built apparently in the days of the Emperor Gallienus. Its greatest diameter is 226 feet and its smallest 166. It is a ruin without any beauty. The main door, even from the front, looks like a church whose roof has been destroyed by fire. After the entrance door come other doors, cut into thick walls built of little square stones and separated at short intervals by rows of bricks that are usually three bricks deep. Bricks, made of a layer of stone and an equally deep layer of bricks, also fit into the semicircular arches over doors and windows. A great deal of mortar, almost two-thirds of an inch, has been used between each layer. True, this mortar, which I struck with my cane, has become harder than the brick and even harder than the stone.

*Bordeaux: the Palais Gallien*

The ground floor of this amphitheater is Tuscan in type, with four galleries, one above the other, extending around it. (See: *Memoires de l'Académie des Belles-Lettres XII, 259;* there are some good engravings). The Palais Gallien has suffered greatly since the time those memoirs were written. I have never seen such an ugly ancient ruin; it is uglier than the pyramid in Vienna. The two horns of the magnificent crescent that the city of Bordeaux forms around the Garonne, face toward the east. The city lies on the west bank of the Garonne which runs from south to north. The word "runs" is not quite correct for half the time the tide, rising rapidly, causes the Garonne to flow from north to south. On this rising tide all the ships coming from the mouth of the river, ride toward Royan and the Tour de Cordouan.

Business matters obliged me to spend a few hours at Port-Vendres.

On Sunday, March 25th, after eight hours of rain from the west wind, toward late afternoon the weather cleared. At five o'clock I embarked on the steamboat that goes up the Garonne as far as Agen. Large trees lining the banks east of the bridge made a pretty sight.

Magnificent weather on the river. Fine view of peaceful countryside from the cabin on the boat where I took shelter from the sun which is bad for me, and from the din of the embarking. As the tide is rising, the river is now flowing towards Agen. This evening, they say, it will be high tide. Fine view of the hillside above the bridge, almost as fine as the Lormont hillside below les Chartrons. Leaning out of the window I discovered what for me is the height of physical well-being: air warm enough to make staying out-of-doors an extreme pleasure. Last evening it was chilly. Pretty mills, reflecting the rays of the setting sun between tall trees forty years old that crown the series of hillocks east of the Garonne. When I boarded the boat I was received by the cook who was polite and obliging in striking contrast to the manners in this Garonne region where every man thinks first of himself and what he can gain. My traveling companions were out and out Gascons and, even worse, they were vulgar and boastful, talking about themselves and their exploits, addressing their remarks to the cook in an outrageous manner.

An exception was the driver of the stagecoach from Bordeaux to Agen and Toulouse: he was Flemish, a good fellow from Aix-la-Chapelle. He told us that his father had been ruined by the war of 1794. He had a charming dog named Spitz with whom I played the whole evening. I exchanged a few words with a poor, pale young man who had the most beautiful face (beauty *à la* Craven; he looked like the head of Werther in the Sévelinges edition). He appeared to be very tubercular and was hoping that the air of his home town would restore his health. He was returning from the swamps of the Vendée where he had had a job in the vicinity. His is the type of beauty of those heads done by Canova; almost almond-shaped eyes and very little space between the nose and the mouth. I tried to bolster this poor sufferer's hopes; he had had fever every day since December. As far as I could see, he did not make one gesture or speak one word like the gestures and words of the seven or eight other passengers in first class. I made this journey in September, 1828, when I went to see the terror (by the Comte d'Espagne in Barcelona) but, as I did not keep a diary, I have no clear memories of it, only delightful but fleeting impressions.

After a fairly good and nicely served dinner, I lingered on deck a long time, but toward midnight the cold forced me to seek my place on the cushions in the cabin. By good luck we were few in number. Imagine the pleasure of quarreling over a place on the cushions with Gascons reeking of garlic!

At half-past six we passed Cambes, five miles from the Bordeaux country. Night fell; the sky was clear. The river bank, which was fairly low, looked like an enormous crocodile, mirrored as it was in the water. The lower part was the same dark color as the part above. Along the banks of the Garonne clumps of elm trees crowned hills dotted with houses. Not until eleven o'clock at night did we reach Langon where we stopped to take on wood. I decided to stay on deck. When the forests are denuded of leaves the sight of the brilliant stars shining through the bare branches makes a strange effect that stirs the imagination deeply. Sparks of wood from the smokestack, partially hidden by escaping steam, looked like so many nebulae. Some of the sparks flew quite far.

One or two soldiers in second class made their way up to first class, singing and swinging their bodies gracefully the way Elleviou does. This eminently French gesture of defiance seemed to amuse them.

*Toulouse: Seen from the Veterinary School*

The next morning the poor young man told me I had chosen the worst place on the cushions. The Flemish driver had seized the best place and he, the handsome young man, had taken the second best. That is the sort of thing that always happens to me. I had been busily pursuing romantic thoughts in the sphere of the possible—or rather, the impossible—, and the steady motion of the boat, the quiet evening, the sky glittering with stars, had all combined to plunge me into thoughts far removed from *a good place on the cushions.* If there had been many passengers on the boat I would have marked my place when I went aboard; then, to make sure of it, I would have gone down early to thwart the vulgar infringements of this Gascon public. That is why I loathe a crowd which does not allow one the delightful sensation of living aimlessly and devoting oneself to the pleasure of writing novels; and I swear that, in spite of my age, I am definitely not dreaming of gold lace embroidery on my coat collar. The first stage in my reverie had been to recite to myself Petrarch's first sonnet which, aside from an error or two in logic, is, in my opinion, one of the most beautiful works created by the human mind.

As we steamed past the town of La Réole, the young man pointed out how much more beautiful the banks of the Garonne are than the overrated banks of the Loire from which he had just come.

At half-past eleven in the morning we passed under the suspension bridge at Tonneins which was crowded with peasant women in red petticoats. It was market day in Tonneins, a word they pronounce here as *Tonin-ce.* The iron balcony in the public gardens was also filled with red skirts. This little town, known for its manufacture of tobacco, is situated on the extreme edge of a rock of soft stone about thirty feet high. The boat stopped to let off travelers at the foot of a flight of forty steps cut in this rock. The town itself stretches out to its full length along the river; its ancient walls at the river's edge are built of layers of brick mixed with stone.

At this point the Garonne makes an abrupt turn to the right avoiding the Tonneins rock and shortly after joins the river Lot, which was extremely high at that moment. I forgot to say that the banks of the

Garonne showed every indication of a recent inundation. Brushwood and twigs, swept along on the water, had clung to the branches of alders and willows eight feet above the water level, and yet many low-lying meadows planted with willows were still under water.

In spite of this, our boat, which drew less than two feet of water, managed to scrape bottom and ground. The little valve, set in under the boat to supply water to the pump, was so badly damaged by this accident that the boat's speed—if one may call it speed at little more than a mile an hour—was reduced to three-quarters of a mile. On board passengers were already predicting that it would be well after five o'clock this afternoon, the usual time of arrival, before we even came in sight of Agen. Though the air was rather chilly, I got a sunburn and my face suddenly felt very hot. The next day my skin peeled.

This delay notwithstanding, we stopped at Porte-Sainte-Marie to take on wood. All of a sudden we saw a large, heavily laden boat that had passed us on its way down river, bearing rapidly down upon us. The crew began to shout as the large boat's prow crashed into the panes in our stern portholes. Our paddle wheels caught in a rope floating on the water and attached to this wretched boat. The sailors hauled it up and cut it in half. The rope ran swiftly alongside, scraping our boat's railing and when the two boats came together, it split. During those four anxious moments, the sailors, wholly absorbed by this unusual accident, forgot about the boiler which, instead of blowing up, fortunately contented itself with setting the boat on fire. The crew, now all intent on putting out the fire, shouted: "We'll have to go back to Toulouse. We can't handle the boat anymore."

The passengers made a rush for the life boat. The steamboat was shrouded in clouds of white smoke. Suddenly we began to move; the crew had managed to put out the fire without emptying the boiler. We were moving, yes, but great heavens, at what a crawl! At that rate we could not possibly reach Agen before ten o'clock at night and they usually docked there at five o'clock in the afternoon!

I was much amused by a rich landowner from this part of the country who sported several decorations. He flew into a rage because some women, who had been washing their clothes in the river, had hung them out to dry on poplars no thicker than a man's thigh.

"Don't let this happen again," he shouted at them angrily from the

*Ancient Walls of Moissac*

boat. Such are the worries of rich estate owners! He was continually raging at those poor devils who were compelled by necessity, and not by caprice, to depend on him. And these landowners, often old courtiers out of favor, have the impudence to quote Virgil and boast of the delights of country life!

What can one do in Agen at ten o'clock in the evening? I went into a café which was filled with country yokels playing cards. They were having a good time; they had a perfect right to be there and they were doing me no harm; in fact, they were even polite to me. And yet I took a sudden dislike to staying in Agen. At eleven o'clock, therefore, I climbed into the stagecoach bound for Toulouse.

I awoke at five o'clock when we changed horses at Moissac. Handsome brick houses. I was charmed; I could even think I was in my dear Lombardy (where Metternich is the only drawback). Beautiful moldings and window frames, etc. Brick really does help to redeem Gallic ugliness. Suitable projection of the roof over the wall—that is always lacking in France. And finally, to captivate me completely, the rue Moissac was bordered by an avenue of magnificent trees. I knew there was a remarkable church here and I shall visit it when I return by mail coach. I was amused by two youths who shared the compartment in the coach with me; they so thoroughly enjoyed talking about themselves that I forgave them for smelling of garlic.

*Toulouse: the Museum*

# ·֎[ Toulouse, *March 28, 1838* [12] ]֎·

Arrived at noon at the Hôtel Casset. Columns, moldings on the façade. Town paved with little grayish-black, kidney-shaped pebbles. Walking as painful here as in Lyons.

Toulouse is almost as ugly as Bourges only the houses here are three and four stories high. However, there are not three houses in a row whose façades form a straight line. Toulouse has a charming museum and a Gothic cloister where a number of Romanesque or Christian marbles have been assembled. It reminded me of that delightful museum of the Petits Augustins, so monarchic, so pious, which in 1818, certain people in their blind stupidity made haste to destroy.

Incredible vulgarity and filth of the common people in Toulouse, the only people with whom I came in contact in the five hours I spent there. How different from Monsieur Baron's hotel in Bordeaux which can be criticized only for smelling of burnt fat! Nevertheless I was delighted to break my journey at Agen on the way to Toulouse. Thirteen hours there and the sight of Moissac at five o'clock in the morning, gave me keen pleasure. I would have thought I was in my dear Lombardy. Beautiful sky, mild air and, above all, houses built of brick with elegant cornices. One or two even had a suitable projection of the cornice below the roof which, according to the present fashion, is considered ridiculous in Paris. In other days it was the usual style. In Moissac, handsome trees with magnificent branches made the beauty of the streets really remarkable. For those trees were truly beautiful even though they were not yet in leaf.

Madame de N. had told me there was a charming portrait of Descartes in the Toulouse museum; and I was extremely pleased with it. It is indeed the young philosopher, not in the least foolish and credulous and even less hypocritical in an effort to gain promotion or to be elected to the Academy, but a philosopher who doubts and whose doubts and anxieties have made him thin and haggard. Madame de N. was quite right.

[12] Toulouse, March 27th and 28th, 1838, plus one morning until nine o'clock. Good Hôtel Casset; good Café Lissençon. Saw Saint Sernin's, the museum, Saint Etienne's, the bridge over the Garonne and the Pyrenees.

Handsome but strange portrait of Henry de Montmorency, decapi-
tated at Toulouse; and of Cinq-Mars who unfortunately wears a conceited expression and has his hair as impeccably curled as in his portrait
in the Palais-Royal. The Cinq-Mars of Toulouse has a truly French
forehead. Very big nose. I was so pleased to see the museum after a
whole month of being deprived of the joy of looking at paintings, that
for two consecutive nights I went to bed without taking off my
clothes.

After visiting the museum, I wandered about the cobbled streets,
but everything I saw was ugly and coarse. If, however, I had gone back
to my hotel, I would have fallen asleep; so I decided to go into a nice
looking barber shop on the pretty rue Saint-Rome northwest of the
Capitole.

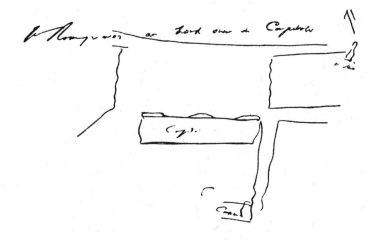

Astonishing rudeness and curiosity of those two barbers!

After leaving their shop, I went to one of the thirty cafés around
the Place du Capitole for a cup of coffee; it was the Café Lissençon,
the best in town. Then, somewhat revived in spite of the pointed paving
stones they have here, I visited the church of Saint Sernin.

Magnificent church with rounded arcades; five narrow naves; the
square piers of the principal nave have attached columns rising to the
vault. Those columns have an imitation Corinthian capital and a completely Greek pedestal. Superb Romanesque church; on all sides semi-

*Toulouse: Saint Sernin*

*Toulouse: the Interior of Saint Sernin*

*Toulouse: Saint Sernin*

circular arches. Façade as simple and as plain as possible; two doors with rounded arches; above, five little semicircular arches with, higher up, a large rose window, though there is no sign of it on the outside. This is the direct opposite of a Gothic cathedral, the cathedral of Amiens, for example; here there are white walls with a series of semicircular windows immediately below the roof.

But on entering Saint Sernin's, what a magnificent sight! I found only two Gothic arches with two blocked windows in the upper part of the vestibule. This vestibule leads only to the extremely narrow center nave, to which one descends by nine steps. The twelve or sixteen square pillars on the side of the large nave have attached columns evidently copied from the Corinthian column.

Noble galleries above the two sides aisles. The spring of the semicircular arches (everything is semicircular and right angles), the windows that open on the center nave from those galleries, are supported by pretty imitation Corinthian columns and are set on a plane parallel to the façade.

Saint Sernin's high bell tower rises from the center of the church on four enormous octagon piers in the transept exactly like Saint Peter's in Rome, except that everything here is narrower. The choir, which begins at those octagon pillars, is embellished with mediocre fresco paintings (which, however, have none of that Gallic ugliness. I barely glanced at them, but they are probably of the Florentine school, XVI century).

These paintings are pathetic. The figure of the Eternal Father, in the vault of the choir, which looks extremely long when viewed at close quarters, but which, when seen from the nave, is restored to good proportions, is by no means ideal. It is simply the portrait of an angry old man of fifty.

This church is very poorly kept; it smells. A few workmen were cleaning the chapels which are decorated with Corinthian columns erected in our day. This is not at all shocking; they harmonize with the imitation Corinthian columns of the original edifice. The very complicated altar has a gilded bas-relief: a galloping bull (the movement is good) carrying off Saint Sernin after the saint has refused to offer him in sacrifice to the gods, who were already becoming decadent. The vestibule ends in a ribbed Gothic vault. Saint Sernin's was completed while Gothic architecture was still in vogue. The first pillar in the church towards the *atrio* has two attached columns. To the right of the façade is a somber brick Renaissance building which lends a little character to this dreary square; on the other side, garden walls.

There was no one in the church where I lingered for two hours, drinking in impressions through every pore. This somewhat consoled me for the two sleepless nights spent without taking off my clothes. In this church I had no feeling of awe, for there are no pointed arches; only a sense of sadness at the lack of width in the center nave.

I went outside to look at the tower; it has five tiers of triangular brick arches. The three lower arches are semicircular, the two upper ones pointed, but the point is a right angle. This church, begun in . . . , was completed in. . . .

The naves opposite windows 4 and 5 are lower than naves 2 and 3. Naves 4 and 5 have windows rounded at the top and opening into naves 2 and 3. More than plain at the entrance, Saint Sernin's, as I have said, has two doors on the south. On the door nearest the clock tower are two ugly lions in bas-relief and two columns with storied capitals in imitation of Corinthian columns. Ten pillars have semicircular arches ending in several right angles, thus separating Saint Sernin's into five naves. I am not counting the two attached columns at the entrance.

The street where merchants gather, rue Saint-Rome, I think, leads to a triangular square, Saint-Trinité, which has a very pretty fountain in the center: a white marble shell supported by three sirens. Here

*Toulouse: Place de la Trinité*

there is an abundance of excellent water. Another square (Place d'Or-léans) has a rather nice garden. Water in Toulouse excellent; this is the only superiority this ugly city can claim over Bordeaux where the water is vile. What is amusing is that Toulouse's admirable water is drawn from the Garonne by a steam engine whose wheels are turned by water from the Garonne. No method could be simpler and yet Bordeaux does not follow this example. Not only does Toulouse water have the same excellence as the water one drinks in Rome, it also has the same faint but agreeable odor.

It is hard to imagine anything uglier than the bridge over the Garonne unless it is the gate at the end and the statue in bas-relief of Louis XIII, erected, I believe, by a battalion of the Toulouse National Guard. Around this bridge, on the left bank of the Garonne, rises the tower of the waterworks which is of average height. The elms in the neighboring courtyard are hideous and look as though they might be eight or ten years old. There are a few handsome trees only where the Canal du Midi joins the Garonne. For the two seas to be joined, the Garonne would have to be navigable from Toulouse to Langon and there would have to be a side canal.

On my way to the bridge, I noticed a very handsome brick church with a number of slender buttresses. It belongs to the artillery regiment of Toulouse which stables its horses in it. I entered the church of the Daurade, so named, they say, because its piers were originally gilded. Today they are covered with immense sheets of black and white marble paper, an ugly sight but perhaps it has some connection with the current Lenten season.

Toulouse is entitled to another good mark: their coffee is hot, a thing unknown in Bordeaux. But in order to be in style the provincial innkeeper serves his coffee in polygon-shaped bowls without a handle, which makes it impossible to touch them. When I asked for a cup of coffee with milk, the waiter brought me a demi-tasse. I explained what I wanted. "Then, monsieur," he said, "you must ask for a bowl."

The table d'hôte dinner was plentiful, but there was no one to serve it and the result was a vulgar and disgusting scramble; each man in turn grabbed the main dish, helped himself to as much as he wanted and then put the dish back in the middle of the table. Incredible vulgarity and what enormous appetites they had! The only pleasant sight was a young Spanish girl with very beautiful eyes (like Pepita, Gina Pietra-grua's[13] sister). She spoke only to her husband—or her lover?

As you enter the street that runs from the Place de la Trinité to the bridge, there are several pretty corniced buildings with columns, all in brick like all the walls in Toulouse. There is even a house with a carya-tid—not bad at all. This is the only street that has a sidewalk, paved, it is true, with sharp little almond-shaped paving stones; but ten or twenty years from now, the city fathers of Toulouse will learn that there are such things as asphalt sidewalks which must have been put into this world expressly for towns that have those beastly little pointed stones. The paving on the bridge is the same. Even the crossing on the Place du Capitole, which is reserved for pedestrians, is paved with sharp stones!

As for me, all day long, I could neither think nor look about me as I walked. It was all I could do to keep from falling and, in spite of my efforts, I hurt myself badly.

The street on which the Hôtel Casset stands runs from the Place du Capitole to the Place Lafayette, an ellipse from which a number of streets branch off. All the houses have two stories and all are the same style of architecture. This square is not bad; the houses are brick color but they are going to be painted light *café au lait* like the Capitole.

The Capitole (façade built in . . .) is the ugliest building imagi-nable, but the rest of the town is so shabby that this huge structure facing a nearly rectangular square, is quite a pleasant sight. It is a palace with a ground floor and two stories above it. There are two projecting wings and a center section, all with angles timidly rounded like those in favor in the century of Louis XV. The center projection has eight columns of reddish marble which stand out awkwardly against a build-ing painted the color of light *café au lait*.

These provincials are amazing. They would feel disgraced if this palace—where, in 1632, the Duc de Montmorency had his head cut off—were to be painted the color all buildings take on after two cen-turies; for instance, the color of the Tour Saint-Jacques-de-la-Bou-cherie in Paris. Perhaps the ugliest part of this façade is the curve of the roof over the windows. A semicircle would have been so noble, but in 1761 the semicircle was considered too staid. Society was mad about

[13] One of Stendhal's many mistresses. (Translator's note)

*Toulouse: the Suspension Bridge*

*Toulouse: Entrance to a Home*

the extravagant style of Abbé Delille.[14] As a result there are twenty-one windows in this building which is crowned by a balustrade as overly elaborate and ugly as the rest of this structure. Between the uprights on that balustrade, you catch a glimpse of the sky through a series of elliptical openings. The projecting wings are topped by groups of warriors painted white, whereas the building is *café au lait*. The group on my right ends in a double-bass *couchant*. I saw only one rather decent object in this entire building: a bust of Napoleon in half-relief which they have had the courage to replace in the center of the triangle supported by eight reddish marble columns. True, they have made his figure too raised and have given him the appearance of a grocer's boy. But, after all, it is surprising to find this bust in a city that upheld the "just and lawful" verdict on Calas.[15]

This palace has a very useful weather vane that shows from which direction the wind is blowing. I shall now allow myself an absurd supposition. Let us suppose that, by some miracle, the city fathers of Toulouse, who are models of all the social virtues, were to become aware of the utter and irremediable ugliness of their Capitole. I believe that at very little expense, they could make it one of the most beautiful buildings in France. Without demolishing the present façade, they would have to put up a brick wall and set it eighteen feet forward, in an exact copy of the *Procuratie vecchie* in Venice. The columns and moldings should be of the same brick one sees in the streets around the harbor. They could be set forward six feet, leaving a third of the façade in the center. At this spot the covered portico would be twenty feet wide instead of only fourteen. They might choose to copy one of the other beautiful palaces in Venice, but I would prefer the *Procuratie vecchie*.

On the north and on the south of the Place du Capitole are a number of very dull but conventional buildings. The hideous houses facing the Capitole jut out over the square. I can forgive the town of Toulouse for those houses because, not only is it not rich enough to

[14] Abbé Jacques Delille (1738–1813): French poet who translated Virgil and Milton, and a clever versifier famous for the ingenuity of his periphrases. (Translator's note)
[15] Jean Calas (1698–1762): Toulouse merchant who was falsely accused of having killed his son to prevent him from becoming a Roman Catholic. He was tortured and put to death in 1762. (Translator's note)

buy them, but if ever it could do so, it would have to enlarge the square on the west to cover all the ground the houses now stand on.

This square is crowded with shops from one end to the other. In one of them I bought three Protestant refutations of the Archbishop's pastoral letter for Lent.

As I came out, I met a peasant woman carrying a peacock in a basket on her head. His splendid tail hung down fully three feet over the basket, his irridescent neck swayed gracefully. The crest on his head was superb. This peacock was surrounded by young peacocks recently hatched which the peasant was taking to be sold. I was overcome with admiration; the colors were gorgeous.

A hundred feet farther on I came upon a little ten-year-old priest in collar, tricorn hat and cassock. His mother was leading him by the hand.

Last night I heard beautiful bells, *bene intuonate* as the Italians say, strike the quarter and the half hours. This morning I was awakened in paradise with all the bells in town ringing the angelus in a succession of liquid notes set at fine intervals just as in Italy. It was really the pleasure that woke me, for the sound was very slight.

I then went to the café where I drank a glass of water comparable to the water of Rome. The coffee was hot. Sensitive and stimulating conversation of several artillery officers, my neighbors at the table on the right. Pitiful nonsense from some citizens at the table on the left. They ended by playing dominoes all morning.

The streets are ugly and very narrow, but even so, today, March 28th, I sought the shade and avoided the sun. What must it be like here in July? From the bridge over the Garonne I had a good view of the Pyrenees. Then as I was on my way to the Saint Etienne cathedral, I saw a sign on one side of the street which read rue Fermat (the name of a famous geometer who is an honor to Toulouse) and, on the other side, the old sign: rue des Nobles. That is a fine commentary on the state of civilization in Toulouse. When I passed through here in 1828, all "the best people" maintained that the Toulouse Parliament had been right to condemn Calas. On this trip, therefore, I have no desire to speak to any members of "good society."

When Saint Etienne's was built they forgot to put in the nave, with the result that the church has this unusual shape:

73

The façade is only a third of a façade. One enters a large square room that opens into the left chapel and half of the main nave of a stately church of Gothic feathered arches.

The main nave is supported by great round piers without capitals. You can see the various ribs of the Gothic vaulting rising from the piers. However, several slender colonnettes, backed against the great pillars, do have capitals, no thicker than a man's wrist, at the point where the pillars join the arches. Thus several groups of vaulting ribs spring from bosses on the great round piers without the use of capitals. The large square room opens against a sort of Renaissance rood screen. Saint Etienne's is, I would think, in the flamboyant style.

As I was looking around the church, I came upon a pretty little garden on the right of the right-hand chapel where trees had recently been planted. There I was quite alone, so I stopped to listen voluptuously to the ringing of the bells. The air was deliciously fresh and I would have lingered there had I not been afraid of being taken for a thief. If an insolent priest had berated me (as had happened at St. André de la . . . to D. de H.), I would have flown into a rage.

Exhausted from admiring and studying intensively so many things, I went back to my room. Wind from the north; nevertheless, standing at a window facing due north, I breathed in the air with extreme pleasure (my room, number 43, Hôtel Casset. Must remember always to engage this particular room on the fourth floor). These loud, rather vulgar people, who pronounce all the end syllables on their words, are too impatient to climb up to the fourth floor.

I understand perfectly the man from Toulouse, who is much more like an Italian than a Frenchman. A woman near me just said: *passegiar*

*Toulouse: Cathedral of Saint Etienne*

for *promener* (walk); the phrase indicates that *pla* means much. People here use very few French words.

As soon as I could summon my courage, I returned to Saint Sernin's which interests me greatly. It is the first Romanesque church to give me a profound sense of beauty. The choir is surrounded by pillars placed close together from which spring arches lengthened at the sides to reach the general level of the arches in the church.

The first saint at the right on the great octagon-shaped pillars supporting the bell tower is *s. Edmundus rex Anglie* (Saint Edmund, King of England); on the left, *s. Georgius* (Saint George). As a rule I do not look in the *Gallia christiana* or anywhere else for the history of a church and, to avoid a plethora of provincial or pedantic nonsense, I read descriptions of it in the *Annuaires* only after I have visited it. Could Saint Sernin's have been painted during the reign of the English, at the same time the churches in Bordeaux were built?

The . . . of the altar, which is very light, is supported by six pretty little Corinthian columns that do not seem at all out of place here. There is nothing sad in this charming church (therefore so little deserving of hell) except the lack of width in the principal nave. Always a bad odor here.

On my way back from Saint Sernin's, tired from my intensive study of a town on which I am passing judgment after only forty-eight hours here, I noticed two statues of saints with necks twisted flat against a curious façade of a church. They reminded me of the Italian words *colle torto*, which mean hypocrite. I went in; a long, square room which has been widened to accommodate the rise of two steps in front of the altar. This church has a great many pictures not nearly as bad as those one sees in the north of France. They are a faint imitation of Guercini, but a thousand miles off, and I probably would not accept any of them as a gift. They are separated by guilded Corinthian pilasters. An old man who came into the church told me it was called Notre-Dame-du-Tour. The Gothic ribs in the dome, plus the elaborate frames around the paintings bear witness that Notre-Dame-du-Tour, though a pretty church, is not wanting in unction. To add to this feeling of unction is the slight enlargement of the back and the altar raised by two steps. Moreover each painting bears a pious inscription in letters of gold not unlike those in a nun's convent church in Rome.

# ·◦〖 Toulouse, *March 29, 1838* 〗◦·

After keeping the coach waiting so that I might take a last look at Saint Sernin's, I left Toulouse at nine o'clock. I did not deign to visit the Hall of the Illustrious at the Capitole; I have shrugged my shoulders often enough in this city which I compare to Bourges. And yet I overheard a remarkable conversation at the saddler's where I went to have a look at the pretty barouche Monsieur L. left in Toulouse for me and which will now take me to Perpignan and Port-Vendres. I was sorry not to meet the three young dandies who came to talk to the saddler about their carriage. Sparkling wit, especially from the blonde young man; rare good sense; charming vivacity.[16]

[16] I ask forgiveness of the reader, undoubtedly a man of means, for the following details which will be valuable in 1880, if, however, this rubbish is still in existence by then.

| | |
|---|---|
| Steamboat from Bordeaux to Agen | 10 francs |
| Dinner on boat | 3.50 |
| Stagecoach from Agen to Toulouse in twelve hours | 11. |
| Excellent room at the Hôtel Casset | 1. |
| Table d'hôte dinner plentiful but table companions unmannerly | 2.50 |
| Demi-tasse | 0.30 |
| Catalogue of the museum, 40 pages | 1. |
| Gift to the caretaker | 1.50 |
| Description of Toulouse | 1.60 |
| Protestant refutation of Archbishop's pastoral letter | 1.50 |

*Canal-Bridge at Agen*

# ··◄[ Agen, *the . . . April* ]►··

From Toulouse to Port-Vendres, I slept most of the time. Arrived in fine fettle and devoted an hour to the curious ramparts of Narbonne, which are a museum of ancient inscriptions and bas-reliefs. On my return, I slept again.

In Toulouse, I abandoned the mail coach, leaving by stagecoach at nine o'clock in the morning for Agen where I arrived at ten o'clock in the evening. Deplorable ugliness and bareness of the countryside from Toulouse to Pompignan. Chateau that belonged to that wretched poet and Jesuit.[17] When he was presented to the Dauphin (Louis XVI, Louis XVIII or Charles X?), the latter recited: "And friend Pompignan thinks he is important." And is in despair!

This Toulouse country has not even a man or a tree to show the unfortunate traveler. I was bored to death and though I did my best to sleep, I had no luck. At such moments I take a poor view of traveling.

And all my books were in my night bag, battened down on top of the stagecoach. Impossible to have the coach stopped. Besides I was so bored I did not have the courage to do anything about it.

[17] Jacques, Marquis de Pompignan (1709–1784): French poet, born in Montauban. Member of the French Academy. (Translator's note)

# ⋅⋅❖[ Bordeaux, *Sunday*, *April 1*, *1838* ]❖⋅⋅

At last glorious sunshine after this abominable, endlessly long winter. We human beings are much more affected by the climate in foreign lands, where we are obliged to form new habits for all the sundry details of life, than we are in our home land.

I do not know to what extent the reader will permit me to talk about the history of commerce in Bordeaux. Last evening at Madame Gir . . . 's, I met an old gunner, a very decent sort, who told me the story of his youth.

Every year before 1792, Bordeaux sent eight to nine hundred ships to San Domingo and the other colonies. The cargoes were always the same and all of them mixed. Most important of all were wines from Bordeaux, brandies from Cognac, flour from the vicinity of Bordeaux, soaps, oils, dried fruits shipped from Marseilles through the Canal du Midi, linens, hats, etc. In a word, once the ship arrived in San Domingo, a planter could go on board and return to his house fully equipped and provisioned. The ships returned home laden with cargoes of sugar and coffee which merchants from Russia, Sweden, Hamburg and all the countries of the North flocked to Bordeaux to buy. There would have been obstacles to prevent sailors from the North from going to the French colonies; and besides, what could they have taken there? Fortunately for young men without a fortune, shipowners were not in the habit of loading their vessels with such trifles as Paris fashions, gloves, etc. . . . Those details were left to the firm's clerks and to the ship's officers.

A young man from Périgueux, Limoges or Bergerac would come to Bordeaux and, with several recommendations, get a job as clerk in a business house. After two or three years in which, by good conduct, he proved his worth (for things move fast in Bordeaux), he would obtain permission to place a small cargo of sundry articles on board one of the firm's vessels. He would then call on one of the merchants who furnished those articles and make his request. The merchant would put him off till the next day and that afternoon, on the Exchange, he would ask one of the heads of the firm that employed the young man for information about him. If the information proved to be favorable, the merchant would readily agree to deliver a job lot to the young clerk, the articles to be paid for six months later on the return of the ship. All the clerk had to pay was a small advance on the shipment.

Thus a clerk, faithful to his employers, could, after ten years' work, accumulate fifty or sixty thousand francs; he would then be twenty-eight or thirty years old. Four clerks, each having this sum or even much less, would then join together and establish a business house. They would buy a ship, hire sailors and officers—and that was the extent of their expense. One must add only the cost of transporting the merchandise which, everything included, wine, brandy, flour, cloth, handkerchiefs from Cholet, etc., was furnished them payable in six months, that is, on the return of the ship. The young merchants insured their cargo. There were firms that guaranteed various purveyors payment of their merchandise at one or a half per cent. They also endorsed bills of exchange payable six months from date supplied by the young merchant-owners of the ship.

In general if the excitement of the game or an inveterate habit of showing off did not turn the young Bordeaux merchant's head, by the time he was forty or forty-five his fortune was made and through the most agreeable work in the world. It is obvious that this way of doing business was quite the opposite to business deals in Lyons. Save for the time when his ship was being loaded, the young Bordeaux merchant did not put in two hours of really hard work. He had to appear on the Exchange and keep up his correspondence with his purveyor.

If he was still poor at twenty-five, the age when before the Revolution a young man married, this wholesale merchant did not marry. Nor did he have the time or the patience to pay court to another man's wife for, above all, he was a gay dog. He therefore became the protector of a young milliner with lovely eyes from the Pyrenees, for young girls were brought to Bordeaux from that part of the country as easily as one brought handkerchiefs from Cholet.

At the age of forty-five, a Bordeaux merchant with a fortune of four to five hundred thousand francs was faced with two choices: to continue living with his mistress to whom he was attached by ties of habit, or to give her ten thousand francs with which she could find a good husband in her home land or in some little town such as Tulle,

Cahors, Figeac, Lectoure or Albi in the vicinity of Bordeaux.

In the latter case, the merchant himself usually married, though late in life as we see; nor did he have many children. As soon as his fortune reached a million, a considerable sum in those days, he began to think of buying a title, *une savonnette a vilain*, a word I heard used constantly in conversation yesterday. After that the merchant retired, built himself a fine house on the rue Chapeau-Rouge or at les Chartrons and lived in honor and glory the rest of his days, quaffing good wine, giving and being given excellent dinners and overcome with happiness when he was complimented by Monsieur the administrator, by the Premier or—the height of glory—by the governor of the province, king of the land, when the court allowed the latter to visit his domains.

The newly titled merchant would then try to place his son in Parliament. Few of the sons of wealthy merchants continued in business. The two hours his presence was required at the office or on the Exchange seemed to the young man an outrageous constraint and he threw himself wholeheartedly into the role of a man about town, a role inherent in this region and one that is still popular.

In an intellectual era, for example a century ago in 1738, a generation of that type would have meant that the country was deteriorating. In an era of hypocrisy and ambitious mediocrity, the sincerity and frankness that are part of the rake's character put the young men of Bordeaux first among the intellectual and moral products of France.

In the middle of the eighteenth century, two main facts struck a sharp key in the melody we have just indicated: wit became fashionable. The Maréchal de Richelieu, for many years governor of la Guyenne and absolute monarch in Bordeaux and who, in spite of Parliament, had had the theater built, proved that something pleasant could be added to good dinners: spirited repartee and the charm of a love affair, neither of which were to be found among "ladies of the night." One day word came from Paris that President de Montesquieu, whom Bordeaux regarded as an average judge, rather lazy and eccentric, was indeed a great man. That made the young lawyers sit up and think. Montesquieu had died in 1755. Ten years later in Bordeaux a group was formed of those eloquent, generous young men so well-known under the name of Girondins, Gaudet, etc. . . . to whom the Bordelais, who have again reverted to being merchants and men about town, have not raised a single statue and whom they have not even honored by naming after them the streets on which they lived.

There is, however, an excuse: the Bordeaux families who lived there in 1792 are no longer to be found in that city today. It is almost as though Vergniaud's contemporaries did not leave any descendants. Those former merchants, now turned treasurers of France, were well aware that, in those egotistical and vainglorious times, no man was a prophet in his own country. After establishing his new quality as a gentleman by leading that noble life for eight or ten years, the only son went into the army or the navy. He then married, but preferably in any city rather than in Bordeaux; he would have found it a waste of time to listen to the anecdotes there.

Now Bordeaux is composed of five[18] different towns:

1. English merchants who keep to themselves exclusively and are not interested in Vergniaud, Valazé and Boyer-Fonfrède, supporters of that Robespierre so anathematized by Pitt.
2. Protestant merchants.
3. Merchants from Mexico, Cuba and Peru who have brought gold to the Palais de Bordeaux and have been extremely useful to it.
4. Merchants from Mauritius and other places in India.
5. Young men, like those before 1792, who came from the South of France, from Perpignan, Cognac and Limoges.
6. And, finally, the descendants of the early merchants of Bordeaux, for the most part now rich capitalists handling, as businessmen, only the most important transactions.

A little of the old commerce still existed in those July days. Fear of a *coup d'état* had already caused business to drop off a third or even a half when Minister Polignac came to power. When the Revolution broke out, everything collapsed. At first Bordeaux did not understand. Certain people led them to believe that Bourbon interests were stirring up a civil war. The firm of Quillar, which underwrote on a percentage basis contracts given to the purveyors by the armorers, was said to have lost several millions.

[18] This is the way Stendhal wrote it, then added the sixth. (Translator's note)

Wind from the north. I have an astonishing appetite. Two and a half hours after eating an excellent dinner at the Café de Paris (2 francs 16, plus 4 sous for the tip: total 3 francs), I felt a great desire to consume the second rice pudding of the day. Sent Monsieur Noël's letter to Monsieur Davizac this morning.

Walked around the fair: small retail trade, third-rate stores. Got a painful corn as the result of yesterday's bath.

The Florentines of today: bored capons.

### Saint Michel's

The Tour Saint Michel, almost opposite the bridge, the highest spire in Bordeaux, is crowned by the telegraph and pitted by bullets like the church from which it is separated by a courtyard. This church, which is completely Gothic, is said to have been built in 11 . . . It has three naves, the one in the middle very narrow, the choir inclined to the left.

Saint Pierre's, on the Place du Chapelet, near that admirable Place Tourny. This seventeenth-century church is shaped like a playing card and has enormous pillars. Nothing could be more commonplace and yet it is so well painted in grisaille that it has a festive air. It could almost be a church in Italy. The façade is not so colorless as the façade of a French church. On this façade there are bas-reliefs three feet high by four feet wide, depicting angels, a touch of the baroque that is not at all displeasing.

A priest was teaching some little boys the catechism and doing it extremely well. He took the greatest pains to make them understand the mystery of the Incarnation; then he questioned the children. They did not answer. The priest very cleverly skipped over the difficult part of the mystery, the formation of the babe in Mary's womb and Jesus leaving heaven an instant later to join his body. One of the children was Spanish, so to make them understand, the priest, a truly eloquent man, drew a comparison between the young Spaniard away

from his native land, and Joseph and Mary on the journey to Bethle-
hem for the census.

Near the second pillar on the right in Saint Pierre's, there is a figure
of a pretty woman, a Madonna, I think.

After we had had the market prices from London and our dinner at
the Café de la Paix, *la Vestale* bored me to death. Madame Pouilly has a
soft, rather muffled voice; Madame Stephen, the dancer, is not lacking
in charm when she is natural and unaffected. She has the body of the
Venus de Medici and is extremely pretty. Seen from behind she has the
demure carriage of a boardingschool girl. Bordeaux is a much more
musical city than Lyons for example.

What a difference in gaiety between the quai de Saint Clair and the
quai de Bordeaux, between the customhouse and the rostral columns!
In Lyons people are devout: in Bordeaux they are gamblers.

A coating of distemper, which spoils so much elsewhere, would go
very well on the estimable arch of triumph on the left bank opposite
the bridge. The rather small stones have been painted with white mortar which spoils the whole appearance. It should all be painted the
blackish-brown color of the stones. The ideal, of course, would be to
cover the attached columns facing the bridge and the pilasters on the
west with stucco imitating marble.

I have just seen a fight between a very shiny black crow and a dog.
The crow attacked the dog, but he was short of breath and, after a
second, flew back to a ring on the end of a pole, his usual perch.

A happy morning; and yet I did not talk to anyone. Madame Stephen's beauty beguiles me; Madame Pouilly's ugliness is incredible; she
is the ideal cook.

Inhabitants of Bordeaux: obvious mixture of the Iberian, the Cimbrian and the Gallic races. Beautiful eyebrows.


## Bordeaux Customs

A Bordeaux businessman sees his wife only at meals. On rising, he goes
to his office; at five o'clock he goes to the Exchange which he leaves at
six and goes home for dinner. At half-past seven, he is off to his club
where he spends his time reading newspapers, talking with his friends

and gambling. Not until midnight does he go home and often not until two o'clock in the morning.

The women spend their evenings completely alone. If a man calls at a house three times in a month, the mistress of the house warns him that he is causing talk about her and begs him on his honor not to call so often. If some of the middle-aged women allow themselves the privilege of receiving, that is because they are protected by daughters who are already grown. It is not the custom for the ladies of Bordeaux to have a certain day for receiving. Five or six women, whose husbands hold high government positions do receive on a certain day in the week, but their salons are little frequented and then unwillingly. The moment the men arrive they begin to play for high stakes and scarcely speak to the women. These receptions are very irritating to the husbands, who are thus prevented from going to their clubs.

Many married men keep a mistress whose house they visit from seven to nine o'clock in the evening. These young women live in little one-story houses, or sometimes in a house with only an entrance floor, but the whole house is theirs alone. Most of these houses are on the boulevards near the church of Saint Bruno, but the young women would much rather have a little apartment in the best part of town to which their lovers consent with difficulty.

This sort of commerce is said to be very stimulating and the strangest tricks are permitted in this game.

A young woman, who receives from her benefactor a fixed allowance of 250 francs a month, in addition to presents, will inform him that she needs 300 francs a month and, if he does not give them to her, she promptly leaves him. The one who is deserted is usually greatly distressed for several days. One thing, however, is obvious: those young women are much happier than the married women, for every day they spend at least two hours with the man who prefers them.

Young unmarried men live by themselves and have absolutely no relations with good women. The few who enjoy tender relations turn to that large class of young women who have protectors. As the protectors are generally very busy men and appear only at fixed hours, it is easy enough to deceive them, but there are not many who do. Most of the young men prefer to have even simpler relations.

Because of their tremendous isolation and the profound boredom in

*Bordeaux: Saint Michel*

which the poor wives spend their evenings until their daughters are grown, their lives are almost like the lives of nuns. If there is a question of someone to console them, a *cavaliere servente*, they choose someone in the house, a choice influenced more by the ease of meeting and a means of avoiding the terrible "what-will-people-say," than by personal qualities.

There are also "grand passions." I am assured that every year one or two pretty women are carried off as they come away from Mass. These kidnappings are in the English style; the lover gives up everything to go away and live with the woman of his choice. As a rule they go to Paris.

The merchant's "friends" are, in general, extremely pretty. They come to Bordeaux from the Pyrenees to be milliners or simply servants. Many of these relations last for the protector's whole lifetime. The cruel part is that as the girls have absolutely no education (the vast majority, for instance, do not even know how to read), when beauty flies on the wings of Time there is nothing left but an excessively boring dialogue.

It is not precisely love that I feel for Montesquieu, but rather veneration. He never bores me by expatiating on an idea I have already understood. This morning when I visited La Brède, I was filled with an almost childlike respect as once before on visiting Potsdam and touching Frederick II's hat that had been pierced by a bullet. This day at La Brède will be a red-letter day in my life; ordinarily a visit to a king's palace merely makes me feel like scoffing.

The property of La Brède where Montesquieu was born, and which he cultivated and increased, lies on the extreme edge of farmed lands on the right-hand side of the road from Bordeaux to Bazas and Bayonne. A little farther on, one comes to that vast desert of sand known as *les Landes*. It is the dreariest region in the world; the water is the color of coffee like the Spree that flows through Berlin and the sand is sparsely covered here and there by pine trees that are scraped for the resin. But even when it has not been scraped, this pine is the dreariest tree imaginable. It has only the name in common with the magnificent umbrella pine that is the glory of the Villa Ludovisi in Rome.

An ancient avenue, planted by the author of *L'Esprit des Lois*, leads to the chateau where he was born; they have just sold some of the trees to advantage. However, one hundred pines are still left on this avenue at the point where the traveler leaves the wretched country road as he comes from the village of La Brède and turns right toward the chateau.

I was all eyes and ears as I caught a glimpse of an almost round building without a façade, surrounded by very wide moats filled with clean but coffee-colored water. That water comes from les Landes and not even fish can live in it. This harsh and gloomy sight reminded me of the chateau where Armide[19] held prisoner the Christian knights she had led from the field of the Crusades.

La Brède is a noble and apparently very strongly built chateau. At the broadest part, the moats are seventy feet wide and thirty or thirty-

---

[19] Armide: one of the heroines in Tasso's *Jerusalem Delivered*. She held the warrior Renaud prisoner in her enchanted garden far from the Crusaders. (Translator's note)

five feet at the narrowest. The water is on a level with the banks and the moats are not deep.

To enter you must cross three drawbridges, passing from one drawbridge to the other between two stout walls pierced by loopholes. Today, those little bridges are made of wood and are stationary. After the first bridge, and directly opposite the gate, is a little island that has been made into a garden no bigger than a hand. It is guarded by three round towers, two of them on the other side of the moat. The waters are held back by a dam; if the dam were destroyed the moats would go dry. Two of the towers defend this very essential dam. The manor walls are not rounded, but form a polygon of perhaps twelve sides. Beyond the moats are a meadow and some wheat fields and then the forest of oaks surrounding on all sides the chateau which sits triumphantly in the center of that great empty space. After crossing the third bridge, you come to a courtyard twelve feet wide by twenty feet long which overlooks the moats. To enter, you pass into a beautiful round tower rather elegantly machicolated. This is the only elegance on the severe exterior of this chateau without a façade. Prudence has obviously dictated the use of narrow windows.

As you enter the little courtyard you find yourself facing a door and windows with pointed arches. A little servant girl, slatternly but not ugly, showed us grumpily into a walnut paneled dining room where everything is ogival in shape, even to the armchairs and the straight chairs. There is no vaulted ceiling but a strangely low ceiling. Passing to the left, we entered an equally sombre Gothic salon, paneled in walnut. But there was nothing grand about this decoration; it was a rather shabby Gothic, like the ogival decorations in the little theaters on the Boulevard. This salon is papered and in good condition. On the paneling I noticed engravings of seaports by Joseph Vernet, thin, scratched engravings that make a poor effect against the dark wainscoting. As the fireplace is high and without a mirror, a modern clock has been hung high on the left on a level with Vernet's marine sketches. Above the clock are two oil portraits, extremely pleasing to the eye for they do not interfere with the general décor. One of those portraits, in an excellent color, is of a pretty woman with heavy eyelids and rather round eyes like some of the women's faces by Sebastiano del Piombo. She is portrayed as the Magdalen gazing at a crucifix, with her hand on

*Château de la Brède*

*Montesquieu's Home at la Brède*

a skull in the shadow. The other portrait is of a terrible warrior with a face fierce enough to frighten children. He wears the court costume of the Louis XIII era. This rather low salon, with only one window, is dark, gloomy, and a good preparation for the adjoining room, Montesquieu's bedroom. Here, so the slatternly servant girl told us, nothing has been changed.

The bedroom testifies to the extreme simplicity of the great man who understood the great painters of Italy and to whom all bourgeois and petty ornamentation was an abomination. This room has only one window though, to be sure, a fairly large one, which faces south overlooking the narrower part of the moat at the point where it is about thirty-five feet wide. It is paneled in a rather light walnut which is by no means impressive. The paneling itself is made of little square panels measuring two feet on the side.

There is a four-poster bed covered in faded green damask. Montesquieu died in Paris in February, 1755, a few months after arriving from La Brède. This bed was, therefore, used for the last time eighty-three years ago. The servant girl repeated that none of the furnishings in this room had been changed. The bed is supported by four very stout walnut posts that are absolutely plain. There is no tester, but a very ordinary and not very high step. Nor is there any mirror above the Gothic mantelpiece. Now the absence of a mirror in this spot is something to which I have never been able to accustom myself; to me it is the last degree of cheerlessness and misery.

Facing the mantelpiece, however, and at a man's height, is a mirror two feet square with beveled edges and a glass frame four or five inches wide; a fashion that was doubtless good taste in the provinces around 1738, a century ago. It is the direct opposite to that horrible pretty-pretty style of Louis XV's court. But the right-hand post on this Gothic fireplace, whose mantelpiece stands fully four or five feet high, is worn by Montesquieu's slipper, for the President was in the habit of sitting by the fire and writing on his knee.

The history of Bordeaux by that good old man, dom Devienne, printed in Bordeaux in 1771, sixteen years after President Montesquieu's death, states that Montesquieu spent the years 17 . . . and 17 . . . at La Brède and it was there that he wrote *La Grandeur et la Décadence des Romains.*

Neither Madame S. nor I could tear ourselves away from this room which, compared with modern luxury, looks plain almost to the point of poverty. Beside the bed is a huge false bronze medallion which appears to me to be a poor copy of the Dassier medallion. Near one window in the room is a terra-cotta bust with its eyes open: it looks like Montesquieu, but the peevish servant girl told us it was a friend of Montesquieu's. It seems to me that the present owner of La Brède could install a professional guide whose wages could be paid by sight-seers, for according to the bad-tempered servant girl, visitors come here almost every day in the summer. The owners might even entrust the guide with one of the volumes from Montesquieu's library that had been annotated by his hand. Our reception at La Brède reminded me that in the past visitors were very badly received at Ferney on orders from the Genevan citizen who had bought Voltaire's chateau. Such successors, living in these celebrated places, keep alive the glory of the great men who made them famous; the proximity of the vulgar offers a contrast.

On the table in the center of Montesquieu's bedroom, is a book containing the names of visitors; the same stupid phrases, the same or-thographic mistakes one sees in the Brocken (Harz) and in Weimar, but no well-known names.

Near the bed is a portrait, very badly executed, of a rather pretty woman with a sweet expression. She is said to be one of Montesquieu's mistresses. I made the mistake of not copying the name which, accord-ing to good usage in the seventeenth century, was on the upper part of the portrait. But I was somewhat moved, I admit, and in this case rev-erie was so sweet that any manual effort would have been too great.

Near the window is a very poor sketch of the statue of Montes-quieu that is in the royal courtyard in Bordeaux and which I have not yet been able to bring myself to go and see; it is undoubtedly a carica-ture of that great man.

The servant girl led us into the library, an immense room, as simple as the bedroom, with a semicircular dome covered by planks painted a light color. This room is possibly fifty feet long by twenty feet wide. The books, in small glassed-in cases are simply bound, the bindings, in my opinion, dating from a period much later than Montesquieu's cen-tury. I noticed quarto editions of most of the good Roman and Greek authors.

Then the servant, grumbling, said: "Someone is waiting for me." A manservant, probably hoping to appropriate our tip for himself, had come in to give her the message.

Above the library window nearest the door are some very bad family portraits; they have been hung against the light and it is probably just as well. Among the portraits are two plaster medallions with hair and beards highly colored which might cost four sous each and which seem to me from a much later date than Montesquieu. Since I avoid all contact with provincial literati and scholars as I would the plague, it is quite possible that I may not see any contemporary portrait of Montesquieu in Bordeaux. He held an important position; he became famous early in life and the century abounded in portrait painters. It is therefore probable that a man with better connections than I have would discover some of those portraits. All the caricatures in the front of the editions of Montesquieu's works that I own are poor copies of the Dassier medallion.

In spite of the servant girl's impatient frowns, we lingered on, unwilling to leave those three rooms a great man had honored by his presence. In the drawing room there is a cartoon of Monsieur Lainé with all his titles enumerated. Nothing diminishes the stature of a dead man so much, especially since the monarchy which invented those titles has been driven out.

Free at last of the servant girl, we made a slow tour of this strange polygonal chateau without a façade. In the moats the coffee-colored water was gently ruffled by the wind.

We returned to the village of La Brède on foot. The streets are wide and irregular, the white houses handsome and built of square blocks of freestone as in Bordeaux and vicinity. The sign BEER over the door of a café attracted us, but there was no beer. However, we found very polite people and when I called attention to the strange architecture of two of their doors, the landlady told me: "This house, sir, belonged to the Templars." The architecture seemed to me to date from the Renaissance.

I went into the church which interested me because of an anecdote connected with Montesquieu. The very pretty doorway has eight or ten semicircular arches flat against the wall. The apse is also surrounded by colonnettes laid against the wall supporting the archways; therefore, a Romanesque church, repaired or finished under Gothic influence. The story goes that Montesquieu carried a book to Mass one day and forgot it. The book was handed to the priest who mistook it for a book of magic. In the middle of several pages were triangles, circles, squares—in a word, the elements of Euclid.

Do I dare to relate the story I was told as I was strolling over a delightfully green field in the shadow of the cemetery wall? But why not? I am already in disrepute for telling people truths that shock the customs of 1838.

The parish priest was by no means old; the servant girl was pretty. People gossiped. This, however, did not prevent a young man from a neighboring village from courting the girl. One day he hid a pair of kitchen tongs in the girl's bed. Eight days later, when he returned, the girl said to him: "Come now, tell me where you put my tongs. I've looked everywhere for them since you went away. That's a very poor joke."

With tears in his eyes the lover embraced her—and departed.

We did not reach Bordeaux on our way back from La Brède until eight o'clock. There had been good news from Martinique so, on rising from the table, we went to congratulate Monsieur G. I have formed a genuine affection for Madame G. Not only is she tremendously witty and unusually courageous—it is not that she faces danger bravely, but that danger does not exist for her—but it would be impossible to find anyone more natural, more completely unaffected. At her house I have met two intelligent gentlemen who were born in Bordeaux shortly after Montesquieu's death. The renowned President was even a cousin of one of these men who owns and carefully preserves the copy of *L'Esprit des Lois* that Montesquieu gave his father. It bears the imprint of Leyden, *chez les Librairies associés*, 1749. The title page carries eight lines of explanations which are rather useless in view of the book's reputation, but which must at least be taken note of out of respect for the author who, in 1748, considered them necessary. This seems to be the second edition for, at the end of the first volume (the two volumes are bound together in one tome) there is an *errata* on one page announcing the changes made by the author from the preceding edition printed in Geneva. The first change is *le ciel* (heaven) instead of *les dieux* (the gods) fourth line in the preface; *Dieu* (God) two lines above.

Aware of my interest, these gentlemen talked to me of Montesquieu, whose son was known as Monsieur de Secondat. A worthy man, but very different from his father, though he lacked the bump of genius he did have a well developed bump of acquisition. The moment he saw fine fruits or any pretty object, Monsieur de Secondat could not resist the desire to take it. However his valet, who always followed him, had orders to pay for everything.

The three pretty little boys we saw this morning at La Brède, who bear the name of Montesquieu, descend from the great man on the distaff side. Among the family portraits in the library is a portrait of a wizened old lady of the Iberian race. In her hand she holds a letter on which I read the date: Agen, September 23, 1723. Montesquieu's family came originally from the Agenois. Madame G. told us that Montesquieu had married off one of his daughters, an extremely clever girl, to a disagreeable cousin from Agen to carry on the family name. Some years later Madame Montesquieu presented him with a son, but because of the sacrifice he had exacted of his daughter, he refused to let the boy bear the name of Montesquieu. The second of the pretty children we spoke to this morning on the stairs inside the chateau opposite the passage leading to the three drawbridges, answered us very intelligently and with great good sense. He should be sent to school in Paris where he would learn about his famous ancestor and be taught that "the nobly born must nobly do."

Those gentlemen, almost contemporaries of Montesquieu, encouraged me to ask them questions. I shall report a few of the stories they told me.

Montesquieu was having a scientific discussion with three or four colleagues in the auditorium of the Bordeaux Academy. As they paced back and forth, each turn brought them near a window beside which stood a vase of carnations. This vase was quickly warmed by the sun.

Unbeknown to his companions, Montesquieu turned the vase and, as they approached the window again, he exclaimed: "Here is something very strange, gentlemen! But, after all, the greatest discoveries often come from chance observations. The side of this vase of carnations that is in the shade is boiling hot and the side exposed to the sun is cold."

The provincial scholars took the matter seriously. They discussed it pro and con and, what is more, they even explained it. At last, afraid of wounding their pride, Montesquieu hastened to confess his joke.

One day he was walking around the town with Madame Montesquieu, an excellent woman of rare good sense, who enjoyed his full esteem. "Here we are at Madame de . . .'s door," he said. "I'm going to go in for a moment. Just wait for me a second." Three hours passed and at last Montesquieu appeared. He had completely forgotten his wife! A case of sheer absent-mindedness and not discourtesy. The annoying part was that the lady he had called on was rumored to be his mistress.

Montesquieu was notoriously absent-minded. One day he went to call on his cousin, the grandmother of Monsieur G. Now it happened that the lady had just had her apartment redecorated and had had steps installed at the entrance to every room. The President had poor eyes in addition to being very absent-minded.

"Oh, cousin," he cried. "You have arranged your apartment in *Do re mi fa sol* and I'm breaking my neck."

As we know, Montesquieu spent two years in England, then settled down for the rest of his life at La Brède. My Bordeaux friend thinks he may have had an income of twelve or fifteen thousand pounds which makes Robert de Marseille's anecdote even more commendable. When absent from home, Montesquieu wrote to his wife only to ask for money. Sometimes a year would go by without a line from him and when at last a letter arrived, Madame de Montesquieu would sigh. As he lay dying, Montesquieu told his children: "My dears, if you have anything at all, you owe it to Madame de Montesquieu."

As Montesquieu did not have a son, he forced his daughter to marry a cousin by the name of Montesquieu in order to carry on the family name. Later on, Madame de Montesquieu presented him with a son, but out of consideration for the sacrifice he had demanded of his daughter, he refused to let the boy bear the name of his barony and the son was known as Monsieur de Secondat. The only thing this son inherited from his father was his absent-mindedness. Walking around the market place, Monsieur de Secondat would pick up all the fine fruit he saw, eat it and leave without paying for it, but his manservant, who followed him, had orders to pay for everything.

A certain Monsieur Latapie had lived from his youth in Montesquieu's household and had been his secretary. I was told that before Montesquieu died Latapie gave the publishers some of the great man's works, a few insignificant odds and ends, as for instance, *Arsace et Isménie*. After Montesquieu's death, this same Monsieur Latapie became a professor of botany and Greek.

## S. Thalberg Concert

The great rule in Paris: do the opposite of what people expect, and as
soon as the conversation turns on the end of the world, the origins of
the human race and other incomprehensible subjects say the opposite of
what Voltaire says. This rule has not yet penetrated as far as Bordeaux.
Actually, a thing I scarcely dare to write and of which, perhaps, a
longer sojourn would undeceive me, is that there is much genuine good
nature and naturalness in Bordeaux. Notice that this is the naturalness
of a human being who, above all, is self-reliant and enjoys talking about
the fine things he has done. This trait, it seems to me, is instinctive from
Bordeaux to Perpignan.

## History of Bordeaux

I admit that I never attach any importance to what is said about the
history of the Middle Ages. I see no certainty save in the principal facts
and those facts lack character; the painters who passed them on to us
did not have talent enough to reproduce the personalities and, besides,
they did not even see them. The monk in a monastery, with no thought
but for a warm cell for the winter and good food, calls the king, who
did not found the monastery, a sluggard.

Later on, under Louis XIV, the writers interested in those times lied
to please the King or, like Fréret, to avoid being sent to the Bastille.
That man might have been capable of seeing or speaking the truth, but
on coming out of the Bastille he swore they would never get him again
and he dedicated his life to Egypt.

The writers who followed Fréret did not have his talent, and they
sold themselves in the hope of finding favor with society and the Academy. Besides, most of them did not *see* the truth and their lies were
therefore a sheer loss. The character of the history of France begins
only with those charming memoirs published by that ignoramus Monsieur Petitot.[20] Monsieur . . . of Bordeaux had the patience to collect
everything that concerned his city. In his verses, Ausone, the rhetor

[20] Jean Petitot (1607–1691). (Translator's note)

and an imbecile well worthy of being appointed preceptor by a Roman emperor of the fourth century, supplies a few vague ideas for the description of *Burdigala* (Bordeaux).

During the two centuries preceding Bordeaux's final reunion with France, which took place in 1451 with the treaty of Charles VII, this city was ruled in the English fashion; in other words, somewhat as we have seen it since 1815. The people assembled in council were consulted on all essential matters and they frequently disagreed with their prince. For eleven years, from . . . to . . . , Bordeaux's king and ruler was the great man who lived within its walls.

By joining France, Bordeaux became subject to an absolute monarchy where the favorite made all the decisions and ruled despotically. This was the cause of the city's frequent revolts—an important fact none of those idiotic minions, who have written the history of this city, have ever seen.

Born in this region, which from having a rational government had fallen under the rule of favoritism, it was only natural that Montaigne and Montesquieu should have been all the more exasperated by Bordeaux's blindness to its situation. In Bordeaux men of open minds had not acquired the debasing habit of servility; they had seen Duretête's head exposed on one of the city gates. And only the year before Duretête had been adored by the people of Bordeaux and had been a leader in the city. But the ruler who reigned in Paris could not tolerate the ruler who reigned in Bordeaux. On January 17, 1676, Louis XIV gave orders to tear down the bell tower of the Saint Michel parish, at that time considered the most beautiful monument in the city. Today it is the telegraph office.

In 412, the Visigoths appeared in Gaul and took possession of Bordeaux; they were Aryans and in the true spirit of the Christian religion (which differed in this respect from paganism), they hanged all Christians who did not think as they did. Thus the bishop of Bordeaux perished in 474. The Visigoths discovered the churches of the Catholics, who were heretics in their eyes; they carried off the doors and pastured their animals in front of the altars. A century later, Clovis succeeded the Visigoths and, after the battle of Vouillé, spent the winter in Bordeaux.

Charlemagne ordered the princes and Frank lords, who had perished at Roncevaux, to be buried in Bordeaux and gave them magnificent obsequies, but Roland was buried at Blaye with Turpin, so often and so solemnly mentioned by Ariosto.

Toward 850 the Normans destroyed Bordeaux which had been handed over to them by the Jews in revenge for the atrocious outrages they had suffered. When those terrible Normans obtained la Neustrie in 911, the people of Bordeaux ventured to think of rebuilding their city which was much less beautiful than the ancient city the Romans had built.

William, the last Duke of Aquitaine, was a puppet in the hands of Saint Bernard who, holding the Host in his hands, hypnotized him in the middle of the Mass.

"The Duke, as though struck by a bolt of lightning, falls down unconscious.[21] . . . Saint Bernard approaches, prods him with his foot and orders him to carry out the sentence which God is about to pronounce through his mouth." It was a matter concerning a bishop whom that poor devil William had dismissed. William had not recovered his senses sufficiently to answer Saint Bernard when the latter ordered him as penance to go on a pilgrimage to Saint Jacques. Before he left, William appointed his eldest daughter, Aliénor, as his heir and destined her to be the wife of Louis the Young, crowned King of France. Poor William died on his way to Saint Jacques. Louis the Young and Aliénor were married in the church of Saint André.

Louis was jealous, Aliénor a flirt. The disagreement began in Palestine where that attractive princess had followed her husband. When Sandebeuil de Sansai, whom the Queen loved tenderly, was taken prisoner by the famous Saladin, Aliénor wrote to the Sultan asking permission to ransom him and at the same time forwarded a vast sum of money. Saladin deserves the enormous celebrity novels have given him; he sent both the money and the prisoner back to Antioch. Louis the Young thought that the Sultan was in love with Aliénor. And when that princess, bored with such a husband, suggested that they dissolve their marriage, using their distant relationship as a pretext, he was convinced that Saladin had entered Antioch in disguise and was secretly seeing the Queen.

The royal couple returned to France. However, the famous Suger,

[21] *Histoire de Bordeaux*, p. 22, by dom Devienne, a good man and not a liar.

Abbot of Saint Denis and regent of the realm in the absence of the King, recognized the danger of a divorce and for a while succeeded in preventing it.

Then Henri, Count of Anjou and heir presumptive to the crown of England, came to the court of France and wooed the Queen. "She told him that she was aware of his feelings for her, but that they must be careful to conceal their love until they could appear together with propriety, that he must retire to Anjou where he would soon receive word from her."

That same day Henri bade farewell to the King and the following day he departed. Wise Suger died. Aliénor again talked of divorce. The foolish King wrote to the Pope and obtained permission to convoke a council. Before this Council of Beaugency, Aliénor declared that she had *thought she was marrying a king, not a monk*. The bishops granted the divorce, and the province of La Guyenne was restored to Aliénor. Six months later she married the Count of Anjou in Bordeaux which became English for three centuries thereafter. Saint André's and all the other beautiful churches were built by the English and, equally important, Bordeaux enjoyed a taste of freedom from 11 . . . to 1451.

Under the English, Bordeaux was the happy capitol of a state composed of Saintonge, Agénois, Quercy, Périgord and the Limousin. In 1161, Henri, the husband of Aliénor, added to those provinces Normandy, Maine, Touraine and Poitou. He was as powerful in France as the king. But three centuries of war had reduced the English in Bordeaux and, in the end, Bordeaux negotiated with Charles VII and returned to France. Those wars, as we know, found an admirable historian in Froissart and, before him, Mathieu Paris was not so bad. Nothing could be more entertaining; one is constantly seeing examples of the individual valor of man. Those wars were not like the wars that preceded our immortal Revolution.

Henri gave Bordeaux to his son who was none other than Richard the Lion-Hearted. Aliénor, now jealous in her turn, killed Rosamonde, her husband's mistress, and at last Henri was forced to put her in prison. As soon as he came to the throne, Richard set his mother free.

July 13, 1235, the municipality of Bordeaux was established with full power and the world saw the name of "citizen" reborn. The wars between France and England were almost continual and this, fortunately, compelled the kings of England to deal tactfully with Bordeaux. Henry III of England sojourned for a year in Bordeaux where he spent money lavishly, giving the most brilliant fêtes for his mistress, the beautiful Comtesse de Biarde, with whom he was passionately in love. Finally all that was left to the kings of England were the sandy plains and vineyards on the left bank of the Garonne. To salve his conscience Saint Louis restored the Limousin, Périgord, Quercy and Agénois to them. There certainly was a devout man who could not be accused of hypocrisy.

Finally we come to Edward, Prince of Wales, better known as the Black Prince, whose reign was the glory and delight of Bordeaux. Edward III, his father, sent him to Bordeaux where he ravaged Languedoc, profiting, with English sang-froid, from the jealousy of the French generals who commanded the numerous troops King Jean still had in this province. The Black Prince, so named from the color of his armor, returned to Bordeaux laden with a vast amount of booty.

What can one say of this great man? How restrain our admiration? The battles of Maupertius and Poitiers, before which the Prince could not harbor the slightest hope, are as interesting as a novel and much more so if the reader is over thirty. Read about it in Froissart (Volume I). The events and orations that preceded the battle are admirable.

King Jean, though taken prisoner, fought with rare courage, whereas the Dauphin fled. Jean was taken to Bordeaux and lodged in the Gothic palace of Saint André so stupidly replaced in 1177 by the commonplace building that today houses the town hall. La Guyenne was raised to a principality in honor of the Black Prince who reigned over Poitou, Saintonge, Périgord, Agénois, Limousin, Quercy, Angoulême, Rouergue, etc.

During the eleven years this great man spent in Bordeaux, he lived with all the magnificence of a sovereign. The generosity and nobility of his conversations with Duguesclin,[22] whom he had taken prisoner at the battle of Navarette, are worthy of a novel by the great Corneille.

What a pity not to have room to relate the incredible daring of

---

[22] Bertrand, Chevalier Du Guesclin (1320–1380): constable of France. Fighting under Charles V, he defeated the troops of Charles the Bad, but was taken prisoner at the battle of Auray. Later, as *Connétable*, he succeeded in driving almost all the English out of France. (Translator's note)

Henry de Trastamarre[23] who, disguised as a pilgrim, entered Duguesclin's cell to seek his advice and was saved by the latter from the vigi-
lance of the jailor who almost discovered him.

Jeanne, the Black Prince's wife, rivaled her husband in generosity.
Duguesclin, to whom she gave 30,000 *écus* for his ransom, threw himself
at her feet saying in these well-known words: "Till now, Madam, I had
always thought I was the homeliest knight in France, but from now on
I shall have a better opinion of my person, since ladies deign to give me
presents of such great importance."

The Prince of Wales' heroic wars having depleted his treasury, he
hoped to levy a tax on the entire principality and, as he could not do so
without the consent of the states, he summoned them to Angoulême.
The states examined the infringements and granted his request only
after the Prince had satisfied the assembly's charges. Edward approved
the plans for reform which they presented to him and the states
granted him permission to levy a tax of ten sous per household
throughout the principality of Aquitaine. Thus, from the year . . . all
of southwest France managed to establish a reasonable government and
to have a great man as their king. Happy France could she have been
satisfied to abide by that!

The eldest son of the Prince of Wales died in Bordeaux, a loss his
father took so to heart that his tendency to dropsy, which he had
contracted in Spain at the battle of Navarette, was redoubled. Returning to England, he abdicated his principality of Aquitaine, which he
left in his father's hands. He died at the age of forty. Last year I saw his
tunic, strewn with black fleurs-de-lis like spear heads, on his tomb in
Canterbury.

After the death of this hero, so modest, so generous and so great,
who seems to symbolize the virtues of another age, the history of Bordeaux is pitiful. In 1379, Bordeaux, like a true republic, joined with the
neighboring towns to defend itself against the French. The confedera-
tion was composed of Blaye, Libourne, Saint-Emilion, Cadillac, Rions,[24]
etc.

On the last day of October, 1450, the Seigneur d'Orval rode out

[23] Henri II, Count of Trastamarre, King of Castile from 1369 to 1379. Thanks to
Charles V and to Du Guesclin he was able to keep his throne. (Translator's note)
[24] Froissart, Chapter CCCXLVI.

from Bazas at the head of five or six hundred men on an errand in the neighborhood of Bordeaux. On the next day, All Saints' Day, what is today known as the National Guard of Bordeaux, rode out against him. This troop of almost ten thousand men, full of courage but lacking in experience, was commanded by the mayor and the deputy mayor. Relying on their enthusiasm, the National Guard failed to maintain order. D'Orval took them by surprise, conquered them and killed eighteen hundred men.

In June 1451, Bordeaux entered into negotiations with King Charles VII. The King's ambassadors were the celebrated Dunois, and Poton de Saintrailles, those heroes of the Maid of Orleans' war. Among the ambassadors of the Bordelais we noticed the Seigneur de La Brède (Montesquieu's estate).

In this treaty the absolute monarch made many fine promises, notably not to impose new taxes. Later on Bordeaux rebelled. Louis XI came to Bordeaux in 1461 and, being a sensible man, confirmed the famous treaty of June 12, 1451. But how could the Bordelais fulfill those conditions?

Louis XI had given the duchy of Guyenne to his brother Charles. One day when that prince was dining with his mistress, the Comtesse de Monsoreau, and the Abbé de Saint-Jean-d'Angely, his confessor and favorite, the latter offered Madame de Monsoreau a beautiful peach. She accepted it and gave half to her lover. Shortly afterward, the lady died. The violence of the poison caused the Duke to lose his hair and his fingernails. He died in May, 1470 at the chateau of Ha, and was buried in the church of Saint André.

From the day Bordeaux belonged to France, people moved out in great numbers. But at last, in 1480, the French ceased to interfere with their wine trade with England. So now we come to Bordeaux's famous rebellion under Henry II, that prince who increased the salt tax in contravention to the famous treaty of 1451.

On October 11, 1548, the Bordelais revolted. Moneins, the King's lieutenant in the province, was killed. The city fathers who had been in great fear, behaved exceedingly well. As a good citizen, President La Chassaigne, a relative of Montaigne's wife, behaved even better, and when the people had cooled down, the High Constable de Montmorency, in charge of carrying out the King's vengeance, came within an ace of cutting off his head. The High Constable began by having one hundred and fifty people hanged. One of the leaders of the revolt was burned alive, several had their heads cut off for not having done the impossible; that is, for not having conquered the people while they were united and angry. When the *jurat* Lestonat was condemned to be beheaded, his wife, a rare beauty, threw herself at the High Constable's feet; in fact she did more, but even while she was yielding, the Constable had her husband's head cut off.[25] Moreover, on the Constable's order all titles and privileges of the city were tossed on a flaming pyre.

The Bordeaux rebellion occurred in 1548. Michel Eyquem de Montaigne was born in the Château de Montaigne, a few miles from Bordeaux, the last day of February, 1533. At the time, his father was mayor of Bordeaux. One can imagine how little talk of the monarchy surrounded the youth of this unusual man given to deep reflection, a thing so rare in France.

Montaigne published the first edition of the *Essais* in 15 . . . In 1581 he was in Venice when he learned that he had been appointed mayor of Bordeaux. This was an important post in a city corrupted by conservative ideas and the bilateral contract with the King. In 1585 Montaigne retired from the mayorality. He died in 1592, leaving only a daughter whose descendants own the Château de Montaigne.

I am well aware that the pages I have devoted to the history of Bordeaux—one of the most interesting histories I know—are, however, merely hors d'oeuvres to whet the reader's appetite. Bordeaux waged war for many years against Louis XIV, but I find nothing remarkable in that period except the story of Duretête, the leader of the Bordelais.

A general peace was being negotiated. Gourville, that wily man, showed the treaty to Cardinal Mazarin. "They should have excluded Duretête and the principal leaders from the amnesty," said the Cardinal. "There is still time," Gourville replied. "We need to make only two copies of the amnesty—one to conform to the agreements made in Bordeaux, the other to contain the exceptions ordered by Your Eminence. I will present the second copy to the Bordelais. If they categorically refuse to be satisfied with it, I shall hold to the first copy."

On his return to Bordeaux, Gourville found that the people refused to listen to any talk of war no matter what the price. As a result, Du-

[25] La Faille: *Annales de Toulouse.*

retête was taken prisoner and executed. Here are the words of the Benedictine monk, the town historian, but paid by the municipality and not by the court, a man with no ambitions toward the academy:

"This unhappy fellow was first a butcher and then a process server. His bold spirit had made him more powerful in Bordeaux than the Prince de Conti himself. Naturally generous, he never took advantage of the means Fate offered him to enrich himself. The people, who formerly adored his every wish and who, for a whole year, had carried out all his commands to the letter, calmly saw him led to the torture. They even carried their ingratitude and disloyalty to the point of insulting him in his misfortune. It is said that Duretête felt this blow more keenly than the physical pains he suffered in his last moments."

*Dax*

# ·◦[ Dax, *April 15* ]◦·

The pretty promenade in Dax is on the ramparts. But those ramparts give the army engineers an opportunity to tyrannize over this poor little town. Who would believe that Dax is a second-grade fortress? Who could imagine that, in the present state of friendship between nations and the fear of the King which characterize the year 1838, that only thirty leagues from the frontier—and the frontier of Spain, a country busy getting its political education—people in Dax who wish to stroll about on a summer evening are being harassed?

Through a strange quirk of pride which would take two pages to explain to foreigners, as well as to the French who do not wish to understand, the ladies of Dax complain of not having any social gaieties to brighten their lives in winter; but when they are invited to balls, their pride makes them refuse under the slightest pretext. Story of the ball on Wednesday in such cold weather: As the result of who knows what whim of vanity, there were only eight dancers and one "wall-flower," as they say in this part of the world. But they danced until eight o'clock in the morning.

The Adour, which one crosses at Dax on a wooden bridge, is a very respectable river. Our stagecoach (74 quintals), one of the lighter variety, made the bridge shake alarmingly.

*Bayonne: the Bridge*

# ·◦[ Bayonne, *Monday, April 16* ]◦·

Arrived from Bordeaux at nine o'clock in the morning. Bayonne seems to be a very pretty little town, judging from the glimpse one gets of it from the high, sandy, pine-covered plain we have been driving through since we left Dax. Its bridges and rivers, the masts of its eight or ten ships, and, mingled with them, its many trees all make a very pleasing sight.

As is proper for a fortified town, Bayonne is restricted. One suspects that the land is valuable; the streets are narrow, the houses four stories high and, in consequence, the atmosphere is not at all like a village as in Rheims or Dijon. But if everything in Bayonne is adequate and fairly well arranged for comfort, there is nothing picturesque about it. On all sides one sees small panes of glass dating from the century of Louis XIV. A new house, which has just been built of freestone near an ancient chateau, is in the dullest style of architecture. The cathedral is what the Italians would call *ragionevole*, rather large and rather handsome. It is Gothic and has a nave and two aisles. The panes of glass in the main nave, which is much higher than the aisles, are what is customarily termed handsome; the small panes have very bright colors. Fortunately, the high altar has no *baldachino*[26] which, to my way of thinking, gives it a noble simplicity. But the ribbed piers which adjoin the choir are carefully covered with wood.

Today, another regional feast day, there were many beautiful women with Spanish faces (handsome eyebrows; strongly marked noses, though not too large, and full of character; their faces rather thin, the direct opposite to the German face). But, in spite of my respect for this ensemble of features, I have seen only one decidedly pretty young girl. As in Bordeaux, the women of the middle class and of the lower classes wear handkerchiefs over their heads, which fashion is not without its charm. One corner of the handkerchief, about eight to ten inches long, is left hanging free.

As it rained from ten o'clock until noon, many men were walking

[26] Late illustrations of the Bayonne Cathedral show a thirteenth-century type *baldachino* over the high altar. It may not have been there when Stendhal visited the church or it may have been temporarily removed for some reason in the 1830's. (Translator's note)

*Bayonne: the Citadelle*

in the cloister adjoining the church. It is a solemn and noble cloister, the only thing here that has given me that feeling.

Many of the streets in Bayonne are paved with tiny pointed stones as in Lyons, but here fortunately the main street has arcades on both sides as in Bologna. That is where I took shelter after Mass.

Sign on a shop: *"Almacen,* Paris dresses," instead of *"magasin"* (shop). This Spanish word is used frequently here in that sense. The quays along the Nive and several streets that run down to it also have arcades, which I found very useful this evening in the cold weather that followed the rain.

In 1834 engineers built a handsome fortified gateway along the left bank of the Adour, but a beautiful gateway in military architecture means only that it is sensible. They also lined the right bank of the Adour with a handsome iron fence for the double purpose of preventing the enemy from landing and for keeping contraband merchandise out. This fence also bears the date 1834. I followed the left bank of the Adour, looking for the sea which I did not find (just as at Vannes). The Adour is a beautiful river, as broad as the Seine at the Point-Neuf. I saw the tide rise and ebb there.

The right bank reminds one of the Lormont hillside at Bordeaux. It is a series of low hills covered with pretty groves of trees. Unfortunately, here in the South, they always plant elms. Today, April 16th, they are not yet green, whereas yesterday near Bayonne I saw a chestnut tree in bloom. Very pleasant, however, are the first signs of green which seem to say: "Spring has come, winter is over."

The lower part of the Adour is spoiled by sand dunes thirty or forty feet high and covered with pines, the ugliest tree in existence. Renouncing my hope of seeing the ocean, which is too far away for a traveler who has spent the whole night driving, I sat down on one of those sandy moors. They are incredibly ugly.

Quite simply, as though it was the most natural thing in the world, the sub-prefect handed me a pass for the farthest frontier and advised me to go to Fontarabie. This is the third time on this journey that I have found *simplicity* in a public official. In Paris the most agreeable of them act as though they were doing you a favor, trying to make you feel the importance of the service rendered. I was greatly impressed by

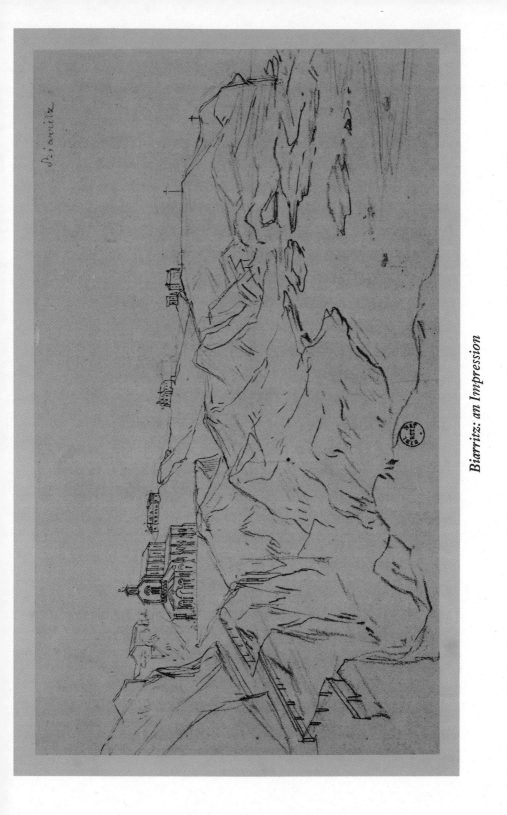

*Biarritz: an Impression*

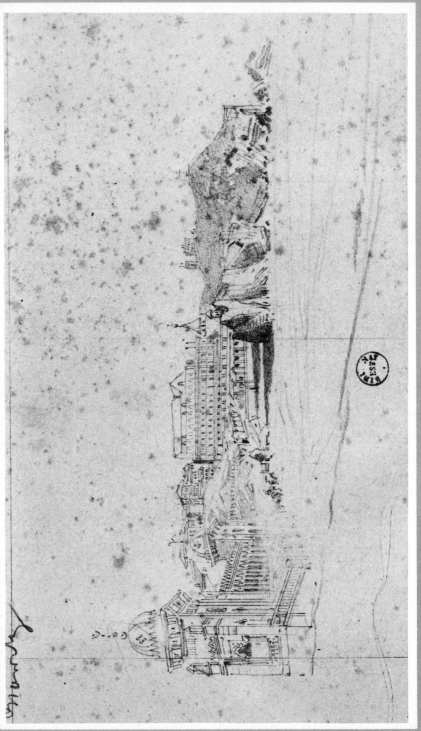

*Biarritz: an Impression*

the unassuming and prompt kindness of this sub-prefect whose signa-
ture I could not read.

I read the pastoral letter of the bishop at the Cathedral. It is not at
all as presumptuous as the Archbishop of Toulouse's pastoral letter. For
that matter, I read it while watching the pretty women coming out of
church. It looked to me as though there was much more religion here
than in Bordeaux.

It is astonishing how few towns in France have a view of the sea.
But after all that is a sensible provision; they cannot be bombarded like
Genoa, Naples, Ancona and Livorno, but one must admit that it is unfortunate as regards the beauty of the landscape. Though I walked for
over half a mile on the sand, I could not catch a glimpse of the ocean,
not even in the distance.

I have killed any number of gnats against the windowpane in my
bedroom. The poor devils were half frozen from the cold and I almost
reproached myself for killing them, but then I thought of the night
ahead. My bedroom at San-Esteban looks out on the rampart and the
fine new harbor. While dining at Mont-de-Marsan I was told that this
hotel is the *ne plus ultra*. However, the Hôtel du Commerce, which
bears the opposite reputation, served a meatless dinner with an enormous fish on Good Friday, April 13th, and of course at the regular
price. We had fasted at San-Esteban on Good Friday.

Yesterday as I came from Langon I saw, for the first time this year,
a poplar tree in full leaf. And, opposite my window, the other side of
the rampart to the west, some thirty Italian poplars are bursting with
green. Swallows skim over two enormous pools of water and this
morning a colony of frogs were croaking there very cheerfully.

To the east of the Place d'Armes, very near the handsome fence that
bears the date 1834, I noticed a square building with arcades on all sides
which is still only up to the first floor. If, as a little child told me, it is a
new theater, there could be nothing more sensible and nothing prettier.
If there are carriages in town, each citizen will be able to have his
carriage meet him under a different arcade and the loading will be done
in a second. In hot weather and in the coldest winters, people will walk
under one of the four rows of arcades, for they would be the coolest
places in summer and the warmest in winter. This is the same plan as
the Moscow theater which the French army saw for thirty-six hours.

*Biarritz: a General View*

All that is lacking is the means to take shelter, but when I raised this objection against the theater in Le Havre I was told: "No one in this town comes to the theater in a carriage."

I found nothing to criticize in the theater in Bayonne which faces westward over the Place d'Armes, the new iron fence and the avenue of handsome trees that border the Adour. To the north flows the Adour and to the east lies the extremely wide quay which has room for all the carriages. It would be hard to conceive of a more fortunate site.

At the end of a street in Bayonne or of an opening formed by the Adour or the Nive, one frequently sees a hill crowned with great trees or a picturesque fortification which the eye perceives at an angle of 20 to 25 degrees.

In Bayonne a demi-tasse costs seven sous, in Bordeaux, six. I had heard much praise of a ridiculous café, the Café du Commerce. Today I tried them all. The best is the Café Américain, though the Café Italien is really quite good for a country café.

Tomorrow, April 17th, I am to be wakened at seven o'clock. I have the first seat in the compartment on the Castex coach which goes to Bidassoa and, I think, to Irun. At this moment the whole country from Bayonne to Montpellier and Perpignan is thronged with stagecoaches in keen competition with each other. For twenty francs a diner at the café was able to get a compartment that had been advertised at twenty-four francs. The companies reduce their prices to lure the traveler away from their rivals.

Forty-five francs from Bordeaux to Bayonne, *Coupé* Dotezac: that is very expensive. The mail coach costs less (here they say *moin-ce, bi-aine* for *bien,* ʃe-*in* for *fin,* and they accent the end of all their words barbarously).

I dined extremely well in Biarritz for three francs. Very decent Bordeaux wine. Extra special for forty sous.

# ·=∮ Béhobie, *April 17, 1838* ∮=·

Last evening in Bayonne I engaged the first seat in the Béhobie coach (five francs). It was due to leave at seven o'clock. The porter was supposed to wake me at six.

After a good night which restored my freshness of perception, always lower after a night spent in a coach, I was awakened by tremendous gusts of wind. It was the wind from the west which had already done me such a bad turn in Bordeaux (around March 21st). Today it brought three downpours so heavy I could not keep my umbrella up.

At half-past six, as there was no sign of the porter, I left the Hôtel San-Esteban and stopped at the Castex stagecoach to ask whether I had time for a cup of coffee. They must have laughed at that question and thought me strange indeed, for they directed me to a disreputable café where I drank coffee at my leisure and then had time left over to smoke three cigarettes.

There was a hilarious young sergeant in the café, who had just finished half a bottle of white wine with one of his friends. The soldiers saw three working girls they knew passing by. All three of the girls were young, two of them pretty with that vivid, engaging and at the same time, modestly coquettish beauty one often finds in Spain. I am at a loss to describe that quality exactly.

How gay the young girls and the soldiers were! The prettiest girl refused to drink.

"When I drink wine," she said, "I can't work any more that day."

The sergeant was in fine form and, to tell the truth, everything he said was excellent. Happy youth, but especially a happy class of human beings! What a difference between this sergeant and his second-lieutenant, a young Parisian from a good background and just out of the military academy of Saint-Cyr. If the sergeant had ambitions for a career, he could count only on his own ability and by no means on family influence and wire-pulling. Had I not been afraid of missing the stagecoach, I would still be sitting in that café.

I came out into a vile rainstorm. It was the rain that had driven the sergeant indoors. An old Spanish soldier offered me a light from his

*Saint-Jean-de-Luz*

short clay pipe; then, with great dignity and without pulling a long face, he asked for alms.

An ill-favored gendarme, an uncouth colossus with a hard face, occupied the second seat in the compartment. He turned out to be a man of good sense, but with the subtlety of a procurer. As nearly as I could make out, he was a paymaster in a regiment, part of which was stationed in Saint-Jean-de-Luz (the 37th perhaps).

He got out at Saint-Jean-de-Luz and his place was taken by a Spaniard who did not greet me when he sat down, but who later proved to be a good fellow. By that I mean that when we finally spoke, at his second retort I felt on a most friendly footing with him, whereas the more I talked to the paymaster, the more reserved I became. The latter was obviously a sly peasant who had come up in the world; in other words, he had risen to the rank of captain-paymaster.

Leaving the city, we drove past pretty little valleys dotted with attractive country houses belonging to the businessmen of Bayonne. There are many rich people here, my captain-paymaster told me. In Bayonne no one has a really luxurious mansion (when I said *hôtel*, my paymaster thought I meant an inn). Even the richest men rent out the ground floor of their house to a shop. Many Jews, my paymaster added.

At last I caught sight of the sea to the right of the road and only a short distance away. This was indeed a real pleasure. So far I had seen it only at a great distance at Pauillac. Tremendous gusts of wind from the west had whipped up a raging sea; the waves were huge and white. The sun was shining, but it rained every hour. I have been subjected to three downpours today and, as usual, it was impossible to keep my umbrella open.

After crossing two bridges, we arrived in Saint-Jean-de-Luz at ten o'clock. Here, on both sides of the harbor, the sea has eaten away half of the town. And what I have seen of the town near the harbor is very strange. No connecting walls between the houses; each house is separated from its neighbor by a space a foot wide. Fires must be rare indeed here.

Shutters have strong hooks holding them out at an angle of 45 degrees from the wall. Several houses have the date they were built engraved above the door; the inscription is in stone and the letters are raised. I noticed a house dated 1670. The windows and shutters are blood-red in color shading into black.

An unusual little chateau, at the corner of the square one passes on the way to Spain, had little square towers cantilevered over the angles on the right and on the left. That was daring.

Oxen, cows, donkeys and horses in this Basque country all seem to be very small, very ugly and very weak. I was told that this was one of the misfortunes of this land. I was also told that the mayor of Saint-Jean-de-Luz has been in Paris thirteen years trying to obtain payment for the plunder the French army took out of the country on their way back from Spain in 1823 and 1824.

If the Minister of the Interior were not so busy with elections, he might consider improving the breed of cattle in this Basque country. For instance, he might send down some specimens and announce that, in 1845 a tax of five sous per head will be levied on any cattle not so improved. He should send them some Swiss cows or some of the Derby stock after first asking Monsieur Arago which would be better suited to the Basque country.

After leaving Saint-Jean-de-Luz, we saw a fine country house on the right with an avenue of plane trees along the roadside. The hills, at first low as one leaves Bayonne, took on more character the farther we went, but they never reminded me of the foothills of the Alps.

On our way to Saint-Jean-de-Luz we saw the mountain of Run or Rhune, the highest mountain in the Basque country. Today, however, great clouds half blotted it out. From Saint-Jean-de-Luz to Béhobie the hills become mountains, though nothing spectacular. As I complained of this, my attention was called to a valley from which, had there been no clouds, we could have seen the snow-capped mountains of the Pyrenees toward Saint-Jean-Pied-de-Port. For a long time I had thought that the *Port Lapice* in *Don Quixote* was a seaport and I could never picture a seaport in La Mancha; I supposed the knight of the sad face to be near Algeciras.

At half-past eleven I came to a street buried among the hills where the houses were all very well built. It was raining. I saw a wooden bridge painted red: the famous bridge of the Bidassoa. To the right of the bridge was an island covered with a greensward that rose barely two feet out of the water. This was the Island of the Pheasants where, so my guide told me, Louis XIV came to be married. This island, which is untouched, is less than one hundred feet long and does not have a single tree on it.

The road makes a semicircle at the wooden bridge over the Bidassoa which runs almost due north and south (perhaps a trifle southeast and northwest). The river is not very broad; and when the *Christinos* destroyed by cannon fire the fortified house of the Carlists at the end of the bridge, it must have made a fine racket in Béhobie. The road is well paved with crushed stone; the houses are very white and solid. On the left of the road is a little ditch lined with little flat stones and facing some houses backed against the hill. Above the row of houses on the east and to the left of the river, the hill is dotted with wooden houses painted dark red.

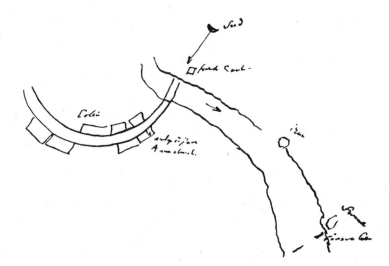

Extreme kindness of the police commissioner who lives in a house on the left at the end of the bridge, a most advantageous situation for controlling these frontiers.

It was raining in torrents. There was no carriage in Béhobie, not even a covered boat, so I set out bravely to return on foot through the driving rainstorm. The wind was so strong I could not keep my umbrella even halfway open. I should have waited, but to me waiting was

*Béhobie: Pont d'Irun*

worse than the rain. Miserable-looking *Christino* soldier whose head I could see at the end of the bridge.

A French major; his fatuous conversation. He talked about his exploits and related a conversation with his soldiers who called him Commandant.

A crowd of sorry-looking soldiers cluttered up the bridge at Irun. As I strolled along the street, I heard someone in a large, ramshackle house singing to the accompaniment of a guitar or rather a dulcimer. Irun is situated on a little hill, which I reached half an hour later, soaked to the skin. Crowd of soldiers and officers in front of the inn. They all had beautiful eyes and they glared at me like wild beasts whose rest had been disturbed. Now I have a high regard for logic and I therefore beg those who may chance to read these lines to forgive this comparison, but I cannot find any equivalent and, moreover, it is exact. The officers and soldiers filled the door of the inn. As I walked past, I nodded to the officers, but they did not return my greeting.

The hotel window faced the little palace of Irun. I have seen nothing in France on this journey that has as much style or that touches me as deeply as this little palace whose five arcades are now closed by a rough wall pierced by loopholes. A similar wall protects the door. On my way to the church I found a barricade still standing. It was made of barrels eight feet high which were apparently filled with earth; you pass through by a sort of sentry post. The walls of the house were riddled by bullets and, from the little Spanish as spoken by Basques that I can understand, I gathered that the Carlists are holding the ridge of a high mountain very close to Irun. On all sides one sees loopholes in the walls and, if I remember correctly, I counted three barricades. This town appears to be in the midst of war, but also in the direst poverty.

Spanish soldiers are completely natural; they never act a part—which explains their poor manner. As it is still rainy, the soldiers on guard carry their guns reversed, with the butt thrust into a sleeve of their iron-gray overcoats. Thus furnished, the sleeve rises two feet above the soldier's head.

As my hotel window looked out directly on the little palace which is now used as a barracks, I could see soldiers at all occupations, even currying favor with two girls selling fruit, or rather herbs, and who—I don't know why—have set up their stand in a new shelter intended for a sentry. I can understand that it is useful for men in the public eye to act a part. I forget which minister remarked to Louis XVI, who did not have the courage to appear in richly embroidered robes: "Sire, a king IS a ceremony."

What is a sentinel without a grim and terrifying manner, or at least an air of relentless duty? Our cavalry sentinels look like Lovelaces, the sentinels of the Imperial Guard like henchmen. The first eight generals, picked at random, would have condemned the Duc d'Enghien, just as the first eight soldiers would have shot down a passer-by at the Emperor's command . . .

As I walked up the street in Irun, with on every side its delapidated houses riddled by bullets, I came to a square where I saw two sentinels and some fifty ugly-looking soldiers standing around in groups. At the end of the square, to the south, was a little palace facing north.

I shall probably be considered a poor Frenchman, but as I have vowed to prefer the truth to a good reputation, I am obliged to say that it is a long time since I have seen anything with as much style or which stirs a man's noblest emotions as strongly as does this little palace. A house covered with forty-franc pieces would have no style in my eyes, but to the eyes of country grocers it would speak a very eloquent language. Ah, well! An enormous building is almost the same as the house covered with forty-franc pieces. It says: it took a lot of money to build me.

In this respect I am such an enemy of my country and such a bad Frenchman that this little palace in Irun gave me much more pleasure than the huge theater in Bordeaux.

This palace has five porticoes with round arches closed by four columns. Above the porticoes is a handsome balcony in a bold, flamboyant style, supported by stones that serve as beam ends. Over each window is a triangle and above that an open space, with ornamentation and rich, rather darkish yellow stones in symmetrical rows. The façade ends in a handsome cornice. Now comes the unusual touch: above the cornice is a balustrade decorated with stone vases from which burst what appear to be stone flames. There is an ornament in the middle of the balustrade, with ornaments at both ends, leaving an opening which is oval in shape. In that oval space, to the left of the spectator, is the clock tower whose handsome gilded frame has been set in the façade, directly below the cornice.

On top of the palace is a large square structure, a continuation of the interior walls, with two semicircular windows in it. That is odd, I admit, but not at all ugly, which perhaps has something to do with the present fortresslike condition of this poor little palace where a hideous supply shop hides the lower part of the portico.

The large mountain one sees in the distance is occupied by Carlists and on three or four low hills around Irun the *Christinos* have built redoubts. On the whole this little palace seems to me to be in the style of Bernini. In Rome I would probably have paid no attention to it; but after seeing Tours, Bordeaux, Toulouse and Bayonne, it gave me great pleasure. The houses on both sides of the palace are conventional in type.

While dining I gazed at this palace and watched the Spanish soldiers, courageous young savages. My supper consisted of a very good bread soup; a good rice dish with chick-peas which, when cooked, look like corn and are tasteless; a slice of bacon wrapped in leaves cut in squares the size of a ten-sous piece. This hay was very bitter; the wine was like ink; a ragout with sauce had such a strange taste that I could not finish my cutlet. A fine dinner for a man who had just walked half a league in a driving rain! Price of dinner: fifty sous. I asked for coffee. "Two *reales*," the landlady told me. It was obvious that I should have bargained with her over the fifty sous but, aside from whether the dinner was worth that much, to haggle over the price at this point would have robbed me of all enjoyment.

When I went into the kitchen to get a light for my cigar, I found the hearth blocked by two soldiers and a stagecoach driver, all in earnest conversation. One soldier very politely took a lighted charcoal from a little brass gadget used for that purpose and held it out to me. Alexandre, the driver of the stagecoach from Bayonne to Béhobie, had brought my heavy coat that far. Now he sent his brother, a stocky young shepherd of fifteen, to carry it the rest of the way.

I made the mistake of not getting thoroughly dry in Irun; I am paying for it today (gout in the tendon of my left big toe), but I was so eager to see everything.

To go to Fontarabie, we turned left on leaving the inn and took the

first street on the left. Many of the houses we passed had round stone
arches between the windows on the first floor and over the doors. They
appeared to be well built and, I dare say, most of them have style;
whereas the houses in Béhobie, though apparently much more commodious, look to me like comfortable farm houses without a shadow of
style. They are pock-marked by bullets—English bullets, my fifteen-
year-old Basque told me. He spoke no French and only a little Spanish.
If ever I return to Spain I must remember to arm myself with the
dialogues of Madame de Genlis. I understand enough Spanish to read
the newspapers, but in conversation I am so intent on what I want to
say that I forget the words. I speak Italian or English to my Basque.

"Monsieur, do you wish to see the church?"

I had forgotten the church which, from a distance, had greatly impressed me. It stands on a hillside on the way down to the Bidassoa,
almost like the church in Fontarabie.

This church is built of medium-size stones, rectangular in shape and
perfectly even, almost like the ramparts in Avignon. They are also the
same charming *café au lait* color verging on yellow. Inside the church
is lined with pointed arches flat against the walls, but the outer walls are
plain and majestically bare of ornament. This is just the opposite of the
Gothic style in Amiens, which did not dare to leave the slightest part
unornamented. The uninhibited bareness of the churches in Irun and
Fontarabie is closely related to the architecture of antiquity.

One enters through a door on the left of the church. I think it is
under the bell tower. I did not make any notes while I was there; it
looked like rain and I was completely absorbed in my impressions. In its
vast empty space the interior is a striking imitation of the boldly unornamented exteriors of ancient temples. It is shaped like a tennis court,
the same shape as the first part of Saint André's in Bordeaux and Notre-
Dame-du-Tour in Toulouse. The flat arches which form the roof are
Gothic with strongly marked ribs, as in Bordeaux; but at the point
where the ribs meet, there is a straight line which greatly diminishes the
number of acute angles and produces several angles that are closer to
right angles. The back of the church is an immense gilded structure,
fifty or sixty feet high and composed of three orders of architecture:
Composite, Ionic and Corinthian. Between those columns are a prodi-
gious number of gilded bas-reliefs. In general, those gilded figures, a

trifle smaller than life though very mediocre, tend toward the style of
Bernini. A little sacristan raised the cloths that covered two or three
richly clad Madonnas.

There is a large arcade in the place where the door usually stands.

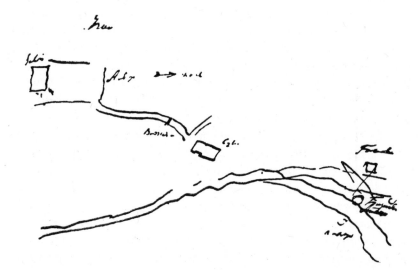

Each altar has any number of gilded bas-reliefs which, at least to my
mind, robs a church of all solemnity. I have been greatly struck by this
fact. It is totally different from the church in Bayonne. I don't remember the year in which the country between Bayonne and the Bidassoa
was annexed to France.

The rain was becoming more and more threatening and I was
forced to leave this church I found so impressive. A throng of street
urchins were playing marbles at the door which is similar to the door of
Notre-Dame in Paris, with many figures, though less ridiculous ones
perhaps, which no revolutionary fury has deprived of their heads.

"Would you like to go across the fields?" the guide asked me.

"With pleasure."

"Irun is small," he told me with truly Spanish pride, "but just look
at the forts!" And he pointed to some buildings on the hillside, around
which I saw piles of earth.

Irun

Three men passed us walking with incredible briskness, very quickly and effortlessly.

"Are they soldiers?" I asked in my garbled Spanish.

"One of them is. The others are smugglers, I think." And, to be sure, they were carrying a kind of double bag that was not very large.

We crossed the Basque fields, walking on little stones driven into the hillside. Some surly dogs showed their very white teeth as we passed through the yards of several houses surrounded by manure piles. Those houses were square, stood alone and looked very solid. That is much better than the thatched cottages in Picardy. I haven't seen a house that looks really poverty-stricken since I left Bayonne.

We met almost no one; although the countryside is cultivated, it looked depopulated. "Bread," said my guide pointing to wheat in a field we were passing. The path was bordered with beans on poles.

All the women here go barefoot and what is even stranger, with the tremendously high wind and the rain that pours down every other moment, they also go bareheaded. They wear their hair in a plait that hangs down almost to the bend of their knees.

When we reached the main road again, the guide pointed out the devastated fields encircled by the last houses. Those fields, which are really swamps protected by dikes that are now being rebuilt, are on the left bank of the Bidassoa. We met three proud-looking men—soldiers.

This morning an officer told me that, in Irun, the Spaniards have a noncommissioned officer in the artillery who is a man of unusual merit. For four years he has been responsible for everything good that his branch of the service has accomplished on this frontier. In addition to the care he takes of the materiel, he is admirable at leading and drilling his men. "Well," the officer went on, "you can be sure they're taking good care not to promote him to second lieutenant."

My fifteen-year-old Basque, who like his brother Alexandre comes from Irun, knows everyone we meet on the main road. I marveled at the proud looks and bearing of two fishermen's wives from a neighboring village. Those women are well aware that love is the main interest of all the men they meet.

# ·≈[ Fontarabie ]≈·

How can one describe the desolate appearance of Fontarabie? Never in my life have I been so struck by the misery that follows war as when I climbed up to this town forty or fifty feet above the plain.

The French and the English have blown up the regular fortifications which have rolled down on the plain in sections as large as half a room. Added to this general effect is an open hole to the left of the gateway. The *Christinos*, or the Carlists—I don't know which—have filled in the most accessible places in these ruins with an ugly garden wall, pierced by loopholes.

Arrived from Béhobie at seven o'clock. In the noise and confusion of departure, I almost lost my umbrella which, last night, the mistress of the house had set aside. A headache had prevented me from going out. Today it was only by chance that I had a seat in the coach. In these stagecoaches in the provinces there is always a free for all. Warning for the future: follow the advice the paymaster gave me day before yesterday and go to Grasse from Marseilles.

The stupid distrust of these Southerners is evident in their refusal to accept two-sous pieces which even public countinghouses accept. As a result there is a scarcity of change. The porter, who brought up my traveling bag was obliged to go to five shops before he could get change for five francs. This morning the paper seller in Béhobie could not change five francs and, as a result, I forgot to pay him. This ridiculous distrust is clear evidence of the violent emotions of these people in the South and of their lack of business acumen. There had been several counterfeit two-sous pieces around, but what does it matter if the bank or the post office accepts them? We are weighed down by the twelve or fifteen enormous sous we are always carrying in our pockets and moreover half of the big two-sous pieces are counterfeit.

All that is left of my journey to write about is Fontarabie and the Dragon of the Gothic in Hendaye. His daughter is a beauty. Another daughter is married to an army officer and costs him plenty of money. He himself is a small tradesman.

Devilish weather from Béhobie to Bayonne. Very sensible conversation among three children, eight to twelve years old. Their precocious wisdom . . . Discreetly dignified replies of a man of thirty. I think they were returning from the Easter holidays. Banter of two twenty-year-old officers on their way from Béhobie to Saint-Jean-de-Luz. A polite Spaniard who entered the coach and stood panting at the door. The other travelers teased him about Monsieur Polignac. His anger. Crowd of *Kesako*.[27]

---

[27] Kesako: ignorant people who keep asking *Ques aco*, Marseillaise dialect for *qu'est-ce que c'est?* (What is it?). This was Stendhal's way of spelling the expression as it sounded to him. (Translator's note)

Arrived at seven o'clock in the morning.

According to those mendacious maps which, like all the stupid works of this century, describe places they have never seen, I had imagined that the route from Bayonne to Pau was along a beautiful mountain road. Far from it! There is nothing to stir the imagination. The road runs straight downhill from one little valley to another with no attempt at an artistic curve, and then climbs uphill in a straight line. The only finesse these drivers in the South know is to put their five heavy horses to the gallop on the downgrade in order to take advantage of the impetus gained and make the first part of the uphill climb still at a gallop. The poor horses are exhausted before they are halfway up the hill and they arrive at the top at a snail's pace.

That is the way things are done in Spain. This stupidity is indicative of the character of these people in the South. Everything is done by fits and starts or on a sudden passionate impulse. The unflagging attention needed to keep the horses constantly at a brisk trot would be too much to ask of them.

In France, the South complains loudly because the North surpasses it in the arts of commerce. The answer is very simple: the South has natural genius, but the North has exceptional capacities and characteristics which insure success in business.

The road from Bayonne to Pau is pleasant, but there is nothing special about it except that it keeps turning to the right. It runs in a straight line for half a mile or a mile, then turns to the right. We left Bayonne at five o'clock in the afternoon in the rain which, with the west wind, has been with us since April 16th (Easter Monday). My traveling companions were a little man with a pointed nose who was wearing decorations and was standoffish, which prevented me, in the left corner of the coach, from having a pleasant conversation with a stout fellow, a merchant from Revel (near the Saint-Ferréol Basin) who occupied the opposite corner on the left. The gentleman with the pointed nose recognized the drawbacks to the situation and was bored; he was probably a high government employee.

We crossed the Adour on the boat bridge between Bayonne and

Saint-Esprit; slippery and fairly dangerous descent; the climb at the end of the bridge *idem*. Apparently the tide was low. The fields around the road have plenty of trees, but I was annoyed not to see mountains.

Two miles from Bayonne there was a chateau on the left. The building itself was uninteresting, but there were large trees massed along the wall in the middle of the road which must make it very pleasant in summer for the poor traveler. In general here, as in the environs of Bordeaux, every fairly prosperous house has a stand of trees of half an acre or an acre along its avenue. Unfortunately those trees are elms, thirty to thirty-five feet high and not yet green. The only chestnut tree I saw between Bayonne and Pau was magnificent and in full bloom. There are many plane trees, often mutilated and trimmed to the shape of parasols as in Nyon or Rolle along the shores of Lake Geneva where they give a very dense shade. A very gay young Béarnaise girl came down from above into the interior of the coach. "Say, are you a police commissioner?" she asked the merchant.

"She keeps her eyes peeled," he remarked to me.

It was dark night when we crossed the Adour. A package of fish had been delivered to the driver and there was a lot of talk in dialect. I knew what they were talking about, but only from my knowledge of Italian—the way I understand Spanish—and not at all from French. Tonight the peasant woman who delivered the fish kept repeating the French word: *Oui, oui*.

At Peyrehorade, which reminded me of Monsieur Mérimée's *Vénus d'Ille*, the merchant from Revel and I had a glass of beer while admiring the ruthlessness of another merchant to whom this wretched "stone-crusher" (that's what they call our coach) brought more than one hundred kilos of merchandise from Bayonne to Peyrehorade for thirty sous. A seat inside the coach costs two francs fifty! It is thirteen miles, so I was told, from Bayonne to Peyrehorade. Gloominess of some dismal little lamps on the walls put there to give this little town a faint light.

At two o'clock in the morning in Orthez, I was amazed at the courtesy of our driver who got into an argument with the Béarnaise girl. She claimed that she had paid four francs for herself and four francs for her mother. But the way-bill showed only four francs in all. I looked the other way. These ugly scenes upset me, which proves that I

*Pau: Place Gramont*

am neither a philosopher like Swift, nor an ambitious person, nor a humorist. In the novels or dramas I admire and reread, I skip hateful scenes; I should like to forget the ugliness of life. The young Béarnaise girl's features were too pronounced, her eyes too close together. They reminded me of the eyes of Archchancellor Cambacérès who, for Monsieur Daru's sake, was so kind to me.

There was not the slightest pride in the long dispute between the driver and the Béarnaise girl, no bitterness, each one simply standing his ground. In the end they appealed to the manager of the coach line at Orthez who appeared, still half asleep and wearing his nightcap on his head. The Béarnaise girl paid and the manager promised to refund the money in two days, after he had heard from the manager in Bayonne. Ridiculous manners of a local citizen, who boarded the coach with his wife and a lot of packages, on his way to Pau. My traveling companion, the merchant, told me he always insists upon having a receipt for his fare. Let this be a warning to me. Last year I paid twice for the journey from Coutances to Saint-Lô.

Between Orthez and Pau I was awakened by shouts from the driver. The stagecoach was climbing recklessly up a mountain at right angles. As there were no curves in the road, the driver was making his horses zigzag and, at each zigzag, he was obliged to halt and shout in order to start them off again. Arrived at the top; without giving his horses time to catch their breath, he put them to a gallop for the descent. This was both stupid and barbarous. I felt sorry for those poor animals; the steam from their breath filled the air.

At last toward six-thirty, the sight of beautiful trees told us that we were near Pau and I woke up thinking of the descriptions I had been given of this city. All of them were false. I had been told of a city surrounded by mountains. We crossed the famous ravine on a bridge and drove down a long street, the rue de la Préfecture. Houses two or three stories high, covered with slate roofs, expensive-looking but not beautiful. (I mean like the beauty *remisso gradu* of Nantes and Bordeaux.) This "beauty" of Pau struck me particularly in comparison with the ugliness of Bayonne. The interior of Bayonne is frequently as ugly as the interior of Saint-Malo and for the same reason—the complete lack of space in a fortified city or on an island like Saint-Malo.

It was cold and damp in Pau at seven o'clock this morning. I was

*Pau: Seen from the Park*

sore and ached all over, because of the cold, I think. Thirty little street urchins crowded around us, shouting: "Shine your shoes! Shine your shoes!" It took an extremely long time to unload the stagecoach. Fortunately I had had the sense to look in my portfolio for the address of a good hotel. I had been so completely mistaken in the San-Esteban hotel in Bayonne that I was reminded of a line of Fabre d'Eglantine's: "And only by sheer luck do I hope to find an honest man."

After an extremely bad inn in Bayonne, I happened on an excellent hotel in Pau—the Hôtel de France in a garden known as the Place Royale. Excellent hotel, excellent tea, good service, courteous, well trained servants, first-rate bed, pretty bedroom. I slept from a quarter to eight until noon. When I feel well, I am full of ideas; I have the situation under control; clouds raised by strange surroundings, bad temper, the need to think of something else—all disappear; my mind is clear.

My plan, therefore, is to go to Marseilles in search of warmth and, if I find it, to take advantage of the opportunity to publish this diary and, in addition, visit La Ciotat, Grasse (recommended by the paymaster) and Aix. Then, when the cold weather is over, I shall come back to Tarbes or maybe even here and then travel by short stages to Oloron, Bagnères, etc., to catch a glimpse of the Pyrenees if possible. So far they look to me rather like pygmy mountains. I crossed them in 1828 at Figuières (one of those days as far as Fontarabie) from one end to the other, saying to myself: *"Pyrénées ubi es?"* (Pyrenees, where art thou?) Tomorrow I go to Tarbes; day after tomorrow, Auch, Toulouse, Carcassonne, Narbonne.

If, when I reach Tarbes, I am still suffering from the cold, I shall press on without stopping, save for a night's sleep, to Marseilles. (I am actually cold as I write this in Pau, between eight and ten o'clock on April 20th.) If the weather is warm, see Arles in detail on the way.

At one o'clock, therefore, I have lunch; then I go out, triumphant.

The Gave at Pau is a fairly broad river since the bridge across it has seven arches. Hard by the Gave is a very narrow hill, perhaps two hundred feet high, on top of which Pau was built. This hill is so narrow because it is crowded by a ravine forty or fifty feet deep at the bottom of which flows a stream that runs parallel to the Gave. This is the ravine I crossed on a bridge this morning on my way here from Bayonne.

Toward the west, at the end of this narrow hill, where the stream

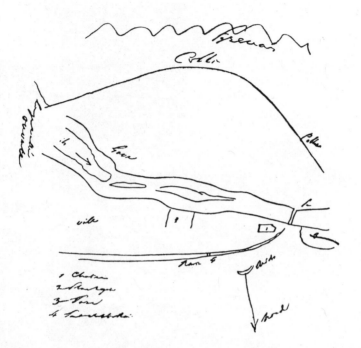

that hides at the bottom of the ravine rejoins the Gave, rises the castle of Henri IV, on a rock one hundred feet high. It would be hard to find a prettier site. As a rule these fortified castles are, like the position of kings, too high to have a good view of what is going on down on earth. This castle, however, is at exactly the right spot. Surrounded by a circle of young plane trees thirty feet high, it has a view to the west of the beautiful trees in Pau.

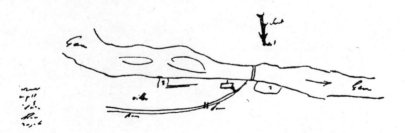

*Pau: Entrance to the Château*

*Pau: the Château*

On the whitewashed gate of the castle garden there is a date, 1586 I think, but it is so badly painted that I mistook the Gothic windows in the gatekeeper's lodge for a modern imitation. Only the shape of the ancient numbers has been cleverly copied.

Without a doubt the château dates from the Renaissance, but it is spoiled by square windows with small panes that reminded me of windows on the rue Mauffetard in Paris, and which rob it of all style. In 1586, sixty-six years after Raphael's death, this is the style that prevailed in the region between France and Spain! On one side I read: "Phoebus made me . . ."

The château is separated from the park by a gorge at the bottom of which flows a stream from the ravine that protects Pau to the north. Twenty peasants were at work digging up plane trees by the roots. It is said that the Civil List is planning to build a bridge over the ravine, which will be greatly widened at this particular spot, and across the Pyrenees road where it comes from the bridge of seven arches to join the castle at the park. One can have nothing but praise for such an enterprise.

I discovered a covered market in a large and useful building directly opposite the Prefecture. It is finished but, great heavens! How ugly the windows are and how pretty this building could have been if the Bourbons had deigned to look at the charming buildings of this type that Napoleon built in Lombardy from 1806 to 1813. His Minister of Finance, a superior man, Count Prina, was massacred in 1815 by Messers. . . . In general those Italian buildings are customhouses. The market in Pau has the advantage of being very large. With 10,000 francs more they could put up a colonnade, which would serve as a covered walk, in front of the façade.

The very ordinary church has a nave, two side aisles and pointed arches. There I read any number of epitaphs in French and all of them full of orthographic mistakes. They date from 1630 to 1640. They are epitaphs for lawyers from the Pau Parliament whose heirs write *Parlemant* with an *a*. Utter absurdity of the orthography of the French Academy: good sense of the Spanish Academy which always tends to spell the word the way it is pronounced.

I strolled along the rue Bonaparte; they failed to blot out this great name and replace it with rue Royale, rue Phoebus, rue d'Henri IV. All

well and good! But what was royalty to Pau or to Grenoble and Aix-en-
Provence? The annihilation of its individual existence. If Henri IV had
been reduced to reigning in Pau, that great man would not have initiated the true policy of France which Richelieu carried on, but after all
Pau would then be something more than a third- or fourth-rate city.

My indignation vanished when I went out this morning and saw the
Place Royale which, from the main street in Pau on top of the narrow
hill, looks south over the valley of the Gave and beyond to some admirable hills with, high above them, the white peaks of the Pyrenees.

Those city fathers who govern the towns of France are, however,
the same everywhere. Below the parapet at the southern end of the
square, they have built baths that are a blot on the foreground and spoil
the view of the Gave and the Pyrenees. As you approach you find
yourself on a level with some chimneys from which smoke is issuing,
but the chimneys are actually thirty feet away. These baths are new.
One must admit that this is the height of stupidity. Notice, too, that by
placing the building fifty paces either to the right or to the left, the
interests of the bathers would in no way have suffered; its position
would have been the same. But no, this building has been placed exactly
on the axis of the Place Royale and it ruins one of the finest views
in France. In my opinion these city fathers in Pau have it all over the
others. They deserve the highest decoration for nonperception of the
beautiful, an Order that numbers so many knights in France.

Thirty years from now when children in Pau, who are ten years old
today and learning to read in school, will be in business, perhaps good
taste in architecture will have traveled by the railroads as far as 204
leagues from Paris. The municipality of Pau will then be very embar-
rassed. They must do one of three things: buy the bath house and re-
build it one hundred paces to the left, buy at least the second floor
which can be made into furnished apartments and rented, or they must
raise the Place Royale eight to ten feet higher.

In Milan there is a committee called *l'ornato* whose duty it is to
prevent the creation of ugly architecture. The mayor cannot give out a
building contract without citing in the preamble of his decree the opinion of the committee of the *ornato*. When the policy of Monsieur de
Metternich (always a friend of ugliness) is not involved, this committee is composed of eight or ten citizens who are acknowledged to be

*The Pyrennees. Seen from Pau*

connoisseurs of the arts. Perhaps in eight or ten years one might try to establish a commission like this in France; their opinion would by no means be binding on the magistrates. But anyone over thirty today would consider a committee of the *ornato* irrelevant.

While I was writing this in Pau around nine o'clock at night, the town was alive with the clatter of private carriages. To me it was an unusual sound and one that had not troubled me either in Bordeaux or in Toulouse. Though the valley through which the Gave flows lies easily two hundred feet below the Place Royale on which my bedroom faces, the rush of that river, a sort of torrent, sounded like the thunder of a waterfall.

Conversation at the table d'hôte of the excellent Hôtel de France was not nearly as dull as the conversation at that wretched eating house in Bayonne. In the first place the dinner in Pau was extremely good, the dinner in Bayonne execrable. In Bayonne the wine was one-third water; here, at least, the wine was good. In Bayonne I had to ask two or three times for a dish; here the waiter was all attention.

In Pau there was only one traveling salesman. He cut his bread with a flourish and plumped down noisily on his chair to show that he felt quite at home. Out of eight men at the table, three were well-bred, including a jolly old gentleman who started a general conversation and kept it going. There was only one conceited fop, making a pretense of good manners, stretching out his arm and helping himself from the dishes before anyone else had a chance. Each of those characteristics stood out clearly.

During those boring dinners in Bayonne, every man's attention was centered on his own interests. There was a girl at the table who protested that they had refused to serve her in her room. "It's extremely unpleasant to dine with men when one is a lady." Most of the men were fifty years old and their conversation was mainly about false hairpieces and the importance of keeping in favor with the ladies!

The table d'hôte in Pau was far above that tone; with the exception of the conceited fop who helped himself greedily and the traveling salesman who, in his anxiety to appear dignified, managed to be merely uncouth and noisy, my other table companions were quite acceptable. Conversation turned on a concert given last evening by the Philharmonic Society. The unfortunate singers are still singing tunes from *La*

*Juive* and making trills on the high notes. Here in Pau, 204 leagues from Paris, that is the last wave of a movement marked by that empty pride which, in Paris, makes the rich and the newly rich flock to the plays of Monsieur Robert.

It seems that the conceited fop is very successful with the ladies. He disapproved vehemently of making jokes about a lady from abroad who, though old enough to be the mother of her lover and fearful lest her charms be insufficient to arouse his passion, received him only after he had drunk two bottles of wine from Champagne.

One of the gentlemen at my table expressed his regret that he was not a member of the club, where he would have been pleased to put me up. Instead I went to a gloomy café that had neither newspapers nor customers. Here the club, it seems, absorbs everything. But the poor café owner was very polite and served me some quite passable coffee. He was even kind enough to have some milk heated for me and all that was very inexpensive. This reminded me of the kindness and honesty of the café owner in Fontarabie.

Tomorrow at half-past ten I go to Tarbes, a journey of ten leagues which they make today in three hours and a half with horses. As I approached the carriage, I saw masses of blossoms falling like snow and covering it. I paid four francs in advance for my seat but was not given a receipt. Tomorrow, therefore, I shall be in Tarbes for two or three hours. Those vehicles, clattering over the streets every quarter of an hour at night and deafening me, may have been stagecoaches and the mail coach, but I did see two private carriages during the day.

Arrived April 21st, in the rain and cold at quarter past three. Left Pau at quarter to eleven; coupé, four francs.

Tarbes, which I figured was in the Pyrenees as it is two hours from Bagnères, is a horizontal town if ever there was one. Through every street two little streams of very clear water flow swiftly. These streams come from the Pyrenees and are perhaps a foot wide and an inch deep.

The sharp, pointed stones that pave the streets are less painful than the paving in Toulouse because in Toulouse they are bare, but here they are covered with sand. (It was so cold, at six o'clock, on April 21st, that I was unable to write.) The space of three or four feet between the stream and the houses could be filled in with asphalt at very little expense and would then be wide enough for a sidewalk. In its present condition this little space is on too steep a slope for a man to walk there with comfort.

The streets are fairly wide, the houses only one story high, the roofs slate. I liked the Place Maubourguet; it is gay, with eight or ten streets opening into it; the river, with very clear water, flows south of it. That river, perhaps eleven feet wide and two or three feet deep in the middle, is merely a larger edition of one of the street streams. It comes into town, I think, through the garden of the Hôtel de la Paix where I am writing this. Running through the garden, as the Po runs through the Ferrarais, it flows between two dikes with the water higher than the gardens which are lower than the dikes.

The Place Maubourguet has one other beauty; the northern part is filled with over forty ancient and very handsome elms, several of them four feet around, one or two of them even six feet in circumference.

*Tarbes*

Arrived at midnight, Sunday night, from Tarbes which the stagecoach left at half-past two in a pelting rain. Had supper between midnight and one o'clock and went immediately to bed. Stomach ache kept me awake. Unpleasant dreams. I had eaten a rotten sole.

Excellent article on Prometheus by Monsieur Quinet in the *Figaro* of the 16th-17th. Took it with me, read it in the Café Dairoles. Cavalry officers (chasseurs and dragoons) there, drinking coffee and playing cards. Listened to stories told by the lieutenant with a handsome face who had been in Algiers four years. From there, I hurried to the church.

I expected to see Gothic run wild somewhat the way it does in Saint Etienne's in Toulouse. Commandant Bergerac's well told but nonsensical tales had prepared me for this. He had talked about the deep religious emotions he had experienced in the cathedral at Auch. But I felt nothing of the kind—in fact, quite the contrary. That servile nature was afraid; he realized this was very bad and probably feared he would go to hell because of it.

The façade of the church has two bell towers like those at Saint Sulpice's with very little space between them for the door. On the towers are two rows of Corinthian columns and, in addition, a row of pilasters which is not as ugly or as dull as one might expect. In the spaces between the Corinthian columns are niches, round and oval medallions and other decorations in the style of the Renaissance.

The interior is almost Greek in its general appearance and absence of gloom. It is not crowded and burdened with details like the great Gothic churches. The architect evidently abhorred the many ugly decorations that were used so lavishly in the year 1200, following the famous principle: if you can't make it beautiful, make it rich.

The nave is wide, the whole effect of the church light, almost gay—therefore, late Gothic, the period just preceding the Renaissance. As a matter of fact this church was begun in 1489 under Charles VIII by Cardinal de Savoie, archbishop of Auch, and it was not finished until the reign of Louis XIV. Raphael had only six years in which to work;

Tarbes: Fontaine de la Bergère

the cathedral of Pisa has been in existence for more than a hundred years.

The outer wall on the left has several light Gothic embellishments. The north door is Gothic, it even has animals, lions or leopards, but toward the top of the door the carved decorations are still unfinished. A rood screen, with eight Corinthian columns, cuts the church vertically in half. This rood screen should be removed and transported, like the façade, to the front of some little church which would be highly honored because of the rich bas-reliefs on the screen.

The main nave, which is very wide, is separated from its two neighbors by four round pillars on each side. These pillars are not too thick and were apparently set up by men who understood how to build a proper column. They are embellished with little half-columns, three inches wide, projecting from ten lines and fifty feet high—a remnant of the usual admiration for Gothic architecture.

Stained glass windows with bright colors! To the peasant who buys colored prints at fairs and the scholar in whom vanity destroys a feeling for true beauty, this is the acme of perfection. What can one say about the remnant of a painting that is not by Raphael or by Michelangelo? And even phrases about those great men are becoming clichés. At the back of the choir above the Lady Chapel is an enormous yellow glass fleur-de-lis. This colossal fleur-de-lis has the age of Louis XIV written all over it.

The chapels bordering on the aisles are separated from them by round pillars, always with little half-columns like those in the main nave. Gothic ribbed arches emerge from those pillars like branches from the trunk of a tree, without the use of abacus or capital. As I was in the church when the noon hour struck and as the sun shone for a second after the rain, I noticed that the building did not face due east but turned a little to the northeast. The arches in the main nave that emerge from the pillars halfway up their height, in other words as high as the aisles, are not separated from the pillars by capitals.

# ··❦[ Auch ]❧··

City admirably situated on top of a little hill. But the hills one sees from the promenade are ugly. They begin toward Rabastens, past a pretty plain covered with meadows bordering on the Adour which we crossed on leaving Tarbes.

Auch was conquered by Crassus, Caesar's lieutenant. Augustus stopped there on his way back from Spain and left behind him a colony that was governed by its own laws and appointed its own magistrates. That was much more freedom than our present constitution grants Auch, but the provinces are so backward that the central government is right to deprive them of the power to make foolish mistakes. A little further on I shall report a conversation I had last evening. From Augustus the city took the name *Augusta Ausciorum* and from that its present name of Auch is derived.

The river Gers flows at the foot of the hill topped by the public promenade, the Prefecture and the cathedral. As everywhere else when respect for law has sufficiently banished fear, a lower town has grown up along the Gers with an upper town reached by a flight of stairs called a *pousterlo* that has more than two hundred steps.

The environs of the public promenade, formed by sloping streets, are very attractive. I attribute that to a good administrator, whose ridiculous face adorns the entrance to an avenue of rather stunted trees. This good administrator's name was Megret d'Etigny. He had a nose like Socrates and the face of Jocrisse,[28] which the sculptors of those days probably considered noble. I could not find a date on the base of the statue which, however, was covered with strange inscriptions, extracts from letters Monsieur d'Etigny had written to the controller-general. This morning I read the prefect of Auch's proclamation on the occasion of the May 1st festival. Nothing could have been duller. Monsieur d'Etigny's letters are reminiscent of the style of that excellent Monsieur de Florian so dear to society in the era of Louis XVI. I must copy a few of Monsieur d'Etigny's sentences which show us a gentleman worthy of comparison with Socrates, save only in vigor. The

[28] Jocrisse: from the character in old farces, fool, simpleton, a henpecked husband. (Translator's note)

*Auch*

statue of this Administrator of Finances and Law holds his plumed hat in his left hand; in his right hand, a horn of plenty and a wheel.

An officer was kind enough to direct me to the best café, the Café Dairoles, on the second floor between Monsieur d'Etigny's statue and the cathedral. Good conversation among officers of the chasseurs and the dragoons who came at eleven o'clock for coffee and to play cards. One of the officers, who had been in Algiers, put new life into the military spirit of a whole regiment. (Incredible uniform the elegant officer Duboin was wearing!)

# ·⚬] Toulouse, *April 25, 1838* [⚬·

I had every intention of not visiting what the Toulousans call, with a certain braggadocia, the *Salle des Illustres* at the Capitole. We know what choices academicians make! Think what the men chosen by the leading citizens of the town must be!

Fate, however, has just made me spend two long hours with those "illustrious men." Forty young men—members, so their poster states—of the Conservatory of Music in Bagnères, gave a concert and announced some highland songs.

After a roll of drums, executed by the regiment garrisoned in Toulouse, the young men appeared, marching two by two like ushers in a theater and carrying alcohol lamps on the end of long poles. They all held their right hands at their sky-blue berets and, as they came down the three or four steps to the Salle des Illustres, they almost fell. The Conservatory uniform is a nasturtium-red jacket with a very effective red belt and the shirt collar turned down over a black tie. All that was not bad; their singing was also not bad. But the music they sang was unbelievably dull and awkward. It would take a genius to think of so much emptiness. Not the slightest hint of a thought! Not a spark of originality! *La Juive* is a work of genius compared to that music! And the words deserve the music. In their songs this evening, Apollo was constantly the subject. His name was mentioned every other moment. When the author wanted to strike a light note, he exclaimed:

> "Were I the master of my fate,
> I would wish to be born
> A gay butterfly."

Those poor young men are credited with singing all those beautiful songs without an accompaniment. Their poster says they are going to Paris. Even if they were backed by all the newspapers in town, a Parisian audience would not tolerate such a conglomeration of platitudes and misconceptions. The only time the author struck a tragic note was when he spoke of a smuggler "who passes in spite of the law."

I could have done without three-quarters of those beautiful songs, but it was impossible to leave; the hall was crowded to the doors. The audience applauded enthusiastically only one solo, the most detestable one of all; but the singer had given us several trills and grace notes which, to the public, seemed very difficult.

The man who taught those poor young men allowed them to sing his own compositions only, not a psalm by Marcello, not a chorus by Weber or by Bellini. All the pieces ended *smorzando*, like Weber's waltz. Now the ceiling in the long Salle des Illustres is horizontal and no one in Toulouse had the sense to raise the ceiling in a room that was to be used for concerts. Before each piece—and there were twelve or fifteen—the regiment band played as loudly as it would between the turns of a conjuror or after the rope dancer makes his perilous leap. At the beginning of every song, the audience at the back of the room shouted: "Sit down!" to those closer to the two poles holding the alcohol lamps. In Toulouse they pronounce *assis* (be seated) *a-ssi-ce*. It was funny: after three or four repetitions of this same routine, I would have been delighted if I could have found some way to leave, but I couldn't think of any.

All the women seated near me were plain. One horrible girl kept pushing her chair back against my knees in her efforts to charm her lover who sat beside her. He obviously adored her. Most of the young men were short but nice looking; they had more style than their counterparts in Bordeaux.

My only resource during those two deadly hours was my opera glass through which I gazed at the Illustres and read the inscriptions engraved on the black marble beneath the busts. The features of those chocolate-colored busts were all alike—which is also the degree of celebrity they enjoyed in this world.

I was seated beside the busts of Messrs. Bunel, Ferrier, Duferrier, de Pins, Saint-Jory, Mairan, Fieubert and Catel. The inscription in praise of the latter seemed to me characteristic:

"As the result of his [Catel's] report and conclusions, which were adopted unanimously by the judges, the famous atheist Vanini[29] was condemned to be burned to death, a circumstance which alone would suffice to make the memory of this illustrious councilor respected."

[29] Lucilio Vanini (1585–1619): Italian philosopher accused of atheism and magic, he was burned at the stake in Toulouse. (Translator's note)

Toulouse has produced two men of note: the celebrated geometer Fermat; but though he was of noble ancestry and a councilor in Parliament, his very excellence apparently proved to be a stumbling block and he was not admitted into the number of the Illustres until quite recently, more than a hundred years after his death. Toulouse also treated the Chevalier Deville, one of Vauban's predecessors, the same way. As for Cujas, the Université de Toulouse, in which town he was born, refused a chair to this great jurist for whom the universities of Bologna, Turin and Bourges competed vigorously.

To the middle class the qualities that constitute genius are highly antipathetic. They demand that their fellow citizens' reputations must first be confirmed by Paris.

I had expected to spend only one night in Toulouse where I had come to pick up my barouche, but I found business in full swing and I devoted three days to studying it. I shall not set down here the memoir I wrote on this subject as I intend to save it for a *History of My Time* which will be published after my death if it is considered good enough. For the present I shall confine myself to saying that speculation is a good thing; the profession is amusing and, for the public, it is an all-powerful remedy against the boredom that is consuming the provinces.

Saint Etienne's, where I spent two hours today . . .

While listening to the missionaries' sermon, interspersed with hymns, I discovered some marble statues of genuine merit on the right and on the left of the choir in Saint Etienne's. There is first the statue of Monsieur de l'Etang, the councilor, in the middle of the choir; opposite it is the Madonna with a charming child. The head has a genuine grandeur, a quality that has long been nonexistent in France. Against the choir wall to the north is the statue of another councilor named de Porta, who had the honor to die in 1520, the same year as Raphael. This is the statue of what is called in the theater a young lead.

I would think that Toulouse has had some connection with Rome. While the many paintings in Notre Dame du Taur are extremely dull, they are not as bad as those painted in France before and even after David, I mean before the present generation. In spite of the tremendous influence brought to bear by the Academy in the century in which Léopold Robert and Eugène Delacroix lived, every artist who has the slightest bit of soul, dares to be himself (save to die of hunger if the Academy assigns the works).

Toulouse has had religion, as witness Vanini and Calas; it also produced a painter, unknown, I think, in Paris. Antoine Rivals, born in Toulouse in 1665, went to Rome at an early age. But what could he find there in 1690? Guido Reni and Guercino were dead. The Cavaliere d'Arpino and other members of the Academy were in power and praising the noble genre fierce Michelangelo da Caravaggio had fought against. Unfortunately the churches that had ordered paintings from Rivals refused to accept them as too ugly.

Ancient Carcassonne stands on a mountain alongside the new town. As I came out of the gate of the new town, I caught a glimpse of the ancient city on a height, but I did not know what it was—apparently a ruined citadel without a single window in it. I saw a little circle—a village surrounded by gray walls and gray itself in the midst of the pale greenery of a treeless hill. The weather was cold, the sky overcast as usual and covered by enormous clouds; the wind was strong and it rained every fifteen minutes.

Attracted by some horse guards who were wearing a sort of beret, I came out of an ugly street and suddenly there I was on a beautiful boulevard with open country instead of gloomy houses before me. Without noticing it I had passed through one of the city gates. And there, at last, directly in front of me was that strange gray fortress at the top of the hill. It looked like a bird's-eye view of a city, such as one sometimes finds in paintings.

Forgetting the Aude I walked toward the fortress on a straight line and came to the banks of the river. I saw the bridge whose massive structure, in the midst of this dreary countryside and in this weather which was even worse than usual, delighted me. No doubt the effect in summer would have been quite different. But now the dirty, depressing banks of the Aude were a melancholy sight. At last I came to the narrow bridge where my main care was to avoid being run down by enormous carts drawn by four or five mules that were coming off the bridge as I was going up.

After crossing the bridge, I climbed up to that ancient city. It was like mounting to the attack. Not even a cat on the steep slope! The walls, perched on a rock and thirty or forty feet high, are strong and forbidding. No sign of a window, nor of a human being. I entered through a little Gothic gate. Silence, emptiness. Streets eight feet wide; tiny little houses showing vestiges of Gothic architecture, but above all an absence of any sign of civilization. Instead of glass windowpanes, oiled paper at many of the windows. At last I realized that I was in a fifteenth-century city. Every good thing that has been done since the year 1500 has been done in the new Carcassonne which I saw down below me a quarter of a mile away.

*Carcassonne*

At half-past nine in the evening I arrived in Carcassonne—rain and high wind. I spent the day on the canal; one sees just as much of the country that way and far better than in the stagecoach. I don't know why I had ever thought the contrary. I went this way in 1828. Monsieur Patin was on the boat.

Outside the walls of Carcassonne flows the Aude, a rather small river crossed by a bridge with ten or twelve arches. Beyond the bridge, on a hill, rises the ancient city of Carcassonne. When the "kindness" of the feudal government had ceased to terrify the people of Carcassonne, instead of choosing a site for the new town alongside the ancient city, they set it a cannon shot away. It is unfortunate for the new Carcassonne that the Aude does not flow through the center of the town.

All the streets here are laid out in a straight line and lead, at both ends, into pretty boulevards planted with plane trees fifty feet tall. These narrow streets are paved with pointed stones but, in the center, as in Tarbes, a little stream of fresh water flows swiftly. The square, with its handsome plane trees, must be delightful in summer—everything in it would be in the shade. Neptune, holding a fish larger than himself and leaning against its tail as a prop, looks like a dancer; but the nymphs, carved in high relief on his pedestal, make a charming picture in the midst of those plane trees which I can visualize in full leaf. The nymphs' heads are poorly sculptured, but their bodies are very good. On the whole it is not far removed from the stiff, dignified sculpture one sees on statues like that of Louis XIV on the Place des Victoires.

But to come back to that beautiful old city of Carcassonne, interesting in such a different way from the new city. For here the traveler has an excellent opportunity to learn what French cities in the fifteenth century were like. As I have said, I prefer to visit cities before I read travel books about them or before I call on my correspondents. It is, therefore, to this habit of mine that I owe my great surprise when I happened to walk through a gate and, looking up, saw the ancient city of Carcassonne on its solitary hill on the other side of the Aude. But surprise turned to keen pleasure when, as I wandered around this fifteenth-century city, I asked for *l'iglesia* (the church) and a young woman with beautiful eyes led me to it. Never perhaps have I felt more keenly the elegance of the Gothic. The interior of the choir of Saint Nazaire (the name of this church as I learned an hour later from a priest in Saint Vincent's) is all in the most elegant Gothic which is even more striking in contrast to the heaviness of the Romanesque nave.

This would have been a more thorough account if I had written it while at Saint Nazaire's; but I was worn out and exhausted, dripping with perspiration, and it was cold.

Arrived from Carcassonne at half-past eleven, in five hours and a half. (Coupé: seven francs.)

This city is as gay as Carcassonne is sad, but it is the home of wind. I have just been forced to give up walking through a short street hard by the cathedral to the north. The wind flung little stones so furiously in my face that I was hurt; moreover, I was afraid of being swept off my feet.

This would be a magnificent church if it were finished. Tremendous height of the choir vaulting. Admirable simplicity and elegance of the ribbed piers. Three extremely wide naves; unfortunately nothing but the choir is finished. The main nave is still to be built. Two archbishops undertook this task for which all the love and fervor that distinguished the thirteenth century were needed.

The part they tried to build is rented to a cooper who prudently shut his door when he saw me about to enter the open court surrounded by half-raised pillars, where he was apparently making his casks.

The entrance to this sublime church is through a little door near the end of the choir. In addition to the two aisles, there is a little rudimentary chapel three and a half feet wide between the pillars in the aisles and the pillars that separate the chapels.

Near the entrance door is the handsome tomb of an extremely ugly knight. It is bare, light and gives an excellent idea of the man who is kneeling on it. On either side of him are two wreathed columns and the decorations are from the Renaissance. But I was unable to learn the name of this good man who was so very ugly.

In the adjoining chapel there is a painting of the guardian angel which is a pleasure to look at. It is difficult to know how to go about seeing this church. The magnificent choir is separated from the nave by a wall in very bad taste that is topped by a sort of wooden gallery, the whole thing from eighteen to twenty feet high. I noticed six little monks a foot high, rather like the monks in Dijon; but the faces of the monks in Narbonne are atrocious, the draperies not too bad.

This cathedral was begun in 1272. The choir, the chapels that form the chevet and the two large towers were finished in 1332. It is under the protection of Saint Just and Saint Pasteur. The choir vault is 122 feet high. The name of the ugly knight kneeling on his tomb is said to be Lasbordes. The two towers surmounting Saint Just are heavy; there is a crenelated wall.

The Robine Canal divides the town in half and takes the place of a river.

The Romans liked the site of Narbo and settled a colony there in the Roman year 534. It was said to be the first Roman colony in Gaul. It is certain, however, that they gave its name to all the region from the banks of the Rhone to the Pyrenees. In the port of Narbonne, today twenty miles from the sea, the Romans assembled the troops they were about to launch against Spain. And there Augustus held the general assembly of all Gaul.

Visigoths and Saracens took possession of Narbonne. Charlemagne reigned there and, after him, the Normans. The title of Vicomte de Narbonne was made hereditary around 1180, after which that city was drenched in blood during the Albigensian Crusade. Since the days of Louis XII, Narbonne has belonged to France.

In 1566, votive tablets, memorials of the blandishments showered by the people of Narbonne on Augustus, were discovered in the foundations of the city's ancient wall. This wall dates from the year 11 of the Christian era; it is in the court of the ancient archbishopry. On it one finds in detail expressions of the most abject flattery:

> Every year, on the 9th of the calends of October, the day when good fortune gave this prince to the earth to rule over it, three Roman knights of plebeian origin . . . will sacrifice victims . . . and on the 7th of the Ides of January, the day on which he began to reign over all the earth, they will entreat him by offering incense and wine; each of them will sacrifice victims.

The second part of the inscription was more interesting to me because it contains the sacramental words of the dedication spoken, undoubtedly, by the priest alone. This shows that this altar had the right of asylum. Those who are interested will find here the laws under which one could dedicate an altar and the conditions under which one could decorate it, add to it, transfer it, and make gifts to it.

*Narbonne: the Cathedral*

When the walls were repaired under Francis I, three bastions were added—the bastion of Saint Felix, the bastion of Saint Côme and the bastion of Saint Francis. In them were placed all the antique fragments collected at that period and classified along two lines.

# ·⊰[ Montpellier [30] ]⊱·

The . . . at midnight I arrived in Montpellier, very tired. I had been bored ever since we left Mèze at eight o'clock in the evening. And yet the weather was superb and a magnificent moonlight flooded the countryside. In times past, the moment I was alone I used to dream of love, of tender and romantic affairs rather than those flattering to a man's pride. Since those days I have become more sensible; I learned what you know—but I learned it slowly—and especially that one must play up to a woman's vanity and above all conceal, as though it were the most baneful advantage, any passion one might feel. If a girl is so sure of you, she will stop thinking of ways to please you.

This fine art has perhaps made me less awkward at times, though I still am to a great extent, but it has robbed me of my charming travel reveries. Now I meditate on the arts and on Napoleon's campaigns. To me this is sad. I see that I have fallen into a period of transition—in other words, of mediocrity—and scarcely will it have slipped by than Time, which moves so slowly for mankind and so swiftly for a man, will warn me that I must depart. I was much sillier but much happier when, telling no one, but already grown and signing my name to official documents, I still dreamt of the passions I thought I was about to experience and perhaps to inspire. The details of a handclasp beneath great trees, at night, would set me to dreaming for hours at a time. Now I have learned, at my expense, that instead of enjoying the experience, one must take advantage of it or regret it two days later. Ah, well! I would almost be willing to become again that foolish innocent, who knew so little of the realities of life, if I could recapture the charming and utterly absurd dreams that made me commit so many follies, but which, while traveling, like tonight, gave me such delightful

[30] Exact dates. Left Narbonne at 11:30 with a tall and dejected traveler whom I did not deign to look at and whom I mistook for an Englishman. He was an elderly Frenchman, a timid and spoiled child, the kind, no doubt, who flies into a rage thinking that this shows character. Left Béziers at three o'clock, arrived at Pézenas around five o'clock. We galloped into town at top speed in eager competition with rival coaches. Arrived in Mèze across the river Thau at seven o'clock. Unsociable dinner; traveling salesmen who felt their dignity was being offended; their terrible manners. Reached Montpellier Sunday evening just as midnight was striking. Beastly room at the Cheval Blanc (Grande-Rue).

evenings and certainly could not offend anyone.

Though I am not unskilled at playing the game, I often scorn to take the field; a mere nothing is enough to make me turn away in contempt. A year later I chide myself for having been so scornful. The feeling of scorn, however, is stronger than I am at the moment and, as if to console me for the unfortunate facility with which I reject what should have been loved, my mind keeps telling me that at a certain age a man must stop loving. This is not true! As long as a man is capable of loving a woman for her charming wit, her perfect naïveté—be she completely stupid or a supreme *poseuse*—as long as he can entertain one utterly absurd illusion, he can love. And happiness lies more in loving than in being loved.

No sooner had we arrived in Montpellier in a hideous hired carriage, poorly lighted by two miserable lamps, then we had to settle accounts with the driver. Settle is a euphemism for paying. Now several of the travelers refused to pay. This ignoble spectacle was too much for me. I find these vulgar details repulsive and I lowered my eyes as before the sight of a heinous deed. Then, instead of enjoying these comic details as Gil Blas would have done, I gazed at the stars and tried to pick out the Big and Little Bear that point to the polar star.

After that the stagecoach had to be unloaded and our luggage collected. This is a moment that brings out singularly boorish traits. But when all is said and done I would rather endure that quarter of an hour and enjoy the sight of humanity along the road. I prefer it to the conversation of my manservant. I shall long remember the famous day from Tarbes to Agen when I heard remarks so naïve I would not have believed it possible had I been told them and yet they were made by people well placed in society.

Toward one o'clock in Montpellier, I was taken to an inn on the Grande-Rue. This morning when I woke, I found that the only window in my room looked out on a street which may well be six feet wide. The house opposite has five stories.

I went out in search of a decent café, but found only pharmacies. To be sure, Montpellier is the home of doctors and, in consequence, of wealthy invalids. All the melancholy, tubercular Englishmen come here to die. At last I overcame my dislike of speaking to strangers and asked some men on the threshold of their shop to direct me to a good café and, in my search for a demi-tasse, I went to some that were truly incredible. Later on I realized that there was not one decent café in Montpellier.

I decided to put up at the hotel that was doing the most business. There, as I had not arrived by coach, a big, gaunt woman received me so coldly that my pride was stung. "But what does it matter!" I said to myself and ordered my trunks sent up to a charming bedroom on the first floor with three windows looking out on the street and on a garden.

Through an indiscreet servant I learned the name of the fashionable café to which I hurried as fast as I could and, my desires being by this time unlimited, I asked for some hot water. In my pocket I had some excellent tea from Kiancha, which had never seen the sea, a present from charming Madame Boil . . . And again I found myself in a repetition of the scene last year in Tours which may have bored the reader. All these towns in the interior of France are alike: the same rudeness, the same barbarous service. In the end I shall have to breakfast on chicory coffee and goat's milk, I think. The butter was not bad, though rather peculiar: it was white and it looked like hair pomade.

The café was directly on the Esplanade; there was a fair in progress and full scale maneuvers in honor of May 1st. Superb sun, but the wind was cold enough to be disagreeable. Nevertheless, I spent two hours watching the maneuvers and very poor they were, I'm sorry to say. The officers were well trained; but the poor soldiers were slack, timid and averse to moving. The cavalry soldiers showed a proper military bearing and were very good. How can I speak courteously of the bad luck I ran into? I found the well dressed population who attended the parade insignificant, petty and, to put it bluntly, very ugly. No doubt I was in a bad mood. A few days later I had absolutely the contrary impression in Marseilles.

This Esplanade is pleasantly situated on a little height that ends at the citadel which Louis . . . built as a detached fort to hold in check the townspeople who were given to revolting. The example of the Italian republics had disseminated dangerous ideas in the South of France which, for that matter, was never so brutalized as the North.

Situated between the town and the citadel, the Esplanade overlooks

*Montpellier*

the country round about. At both ends there is an endless succession of
arid little hills planted here and there with olive trees. On the Esplanade
itself there are little trees with low branches that look too much like the
shape of a cauliflower. They still have no leaves though some chestnut
trees around a lake are covered with blossoms and are charming. If two
or three feet of dirt were removed from the center of the Esplanade,
the public could enjoy maneuvers, races, etc., but perhaps the genii
which is bored in the provinces and tyrannizes over the poor little cities
of the interior would be strongly opposed.

I visited the Fabre Museum which faces the Esplanade and marks
the end of the city on this side. Once upon a time I saw that distinguished Gascon, Monsieur Fabre, at the Countess of Albany's in Florence. His presence there was said to have caused gloomy Alfieri to die
of a broken heart. But then Alfieri was born to die of a broken heart
about something, even if his former friend had not preferred another
man to him. After the Countess's death, Monsieur Fabre came into possession of a fine collection of paintings which he was wise enough to
donate in his lifetime to his native town, Montpellier. For this he was
honored like a god by his patriotic fellow citizens. Several years ago on
my way to the Catalan ironworks in the Pyrenees to see the first iron
we had sold to Algiers, I saw Monsieur Fabre in the midst of his museum and all his glory, *umile in tanta gloria*. He was a fine figure of a
man to be so modest, as one can judge from his bust and his portrait,
both strikingly like him, which are in the main hall of his museum.

This museum is said to have been built especially for the paintings.
If that is so, why didn't they build a round tower with a lantern light in
the center? Instead there are pretty rooms very well lighted by windows that open close to the ceiling, but often the paintings have a
double light cast on them, and all too often the varnish on them reflects
like a mirror. Many of them are hung too high and, to cap the climax,
between the windows above the paintings, someone has painted stupid-
looking sphinxes in colors that are too bright.

Those ever-ingenious provincial architects could not decide to paint
the walls a flat gray which is exactly what is needed in order not to
detract from the colors in the pictures. I hurried to look at the famous
portrait by Raphael of a handsome young man with light hair. Unfor-

*Montpellier: Château d'Eau*

tunately it looked to me to be more painted over even than it was in
1831.

This young man, twenty years old (notice 53) looks as though he
knew what a pretty boy he was, an expression that must have pro-
foundly shocked Raphael's simple and tender soul. "He wears a black
cap on his head: his long, blonde hair is cut square at shoulder length;
his black jacket is tied over his chest with a ribbon of the same color; a
black cloak is flung over his left shoulder and held clutched in his right
hand."

The notice adds: "This portrait, painted on wood, is in Raphael's
second manner."

Beautiful light coming from on high. For the painting, there should
have been a lantern light in the middle of the ceiling and not those
windows that cast daylight from two sides.

Below the young man's ear there is a swelling that is hard to explain.
Only the color of the hand is Raphael's. The flesh tones of the forehead
and especially of the mouth have been awkwardly applied; they are too
fresh to have been painted in 1520. It would be impossible to point to a
similar example of freshness after 318 years. Moreover, the color of the
hand is not the same as the color of the forehead. This portrait irritates
me, whether because of the handsome boy's fatuity and the pettiness of
his soul or because of the artist's attempt to make dupes of us, I do not
know. Is it a pastiche by Raphael or an almost ruined painting that has
been repainted entirely except for the hand? The great name of Raphael is always a little disturbing. Only one of those men long accus-
tomed to see in Raphael nothing but money could decide this question.
I would therefore heed an art dealer's opinion on this painting. I know
a perfectly honest dealer in Florence.

One day he showed an artist a small Giotto.

"I would like to buy it," the artist said naïvely, "for it is divine."

"What! Monsieur! A man like you, without any money? That must
not be. Do me the honor to accept as a loan the small sum of twenty
écus (106 francs). A poor devil like me is not rich."

The artist had great difficulty in refusing this unusual offer without
offending the good man.

A dealer from Bologna or Venice is not a good judge of Raphael. I
would rather call upon the testimony of Count D. from Perugia who,

when he buys sketches by Raphael, wears a cóat with holes at the elbow. But the frames on his numerous paintings cost three hundred or four hundred francs! At Count D's I saw a Saint John by Poussin. It is the most beautiful color by that artist I have ever seen.

But to come back to the Fabre Museum. Facing the handsome but conceited young man is the tall figure of a man with large, hooded eyes. The catalogue says it is the portrait of a Medici, the Duke of Urbino, brother of Catherine dei Medici, that queen who introduced poison into France. This Medici resembles neither Giovanni delle Bande Nera nor the famous Lorenzo, nor the Cosimo who was so amusingly called the father of his country, nor even Cosimo I, the Grand Duke. He wears a black cap trimmed with a gold medal. Over a jerkin of cloth of gold, he wears a dark red fur-lined coat, brocaded in gold with gold embroidery on the wide sleeves. In his right hand he holds a gold jewel; the left hand rests on his hip; he has a dagger in his belt. The background of this portrait is green. "This painting, in Raphael's last manner," adds the footnote, "is painted on wood. Vasari mentions it in his life of the great artist. There are two copies in the *galleria* in Florence."

I realize that, unfortunately, I shall be sharply criticized and all because of the same vice: my absurd love of truth, a trait that makes me so many enemies. For one or two centuries all Europe has believed that the portrait of *la Fornarina* in the gallery in Florence is by Raphael. I believe that it is by a painter of the Venetian school to which I would also attribute this second Raphael in the Fabre Museum.

My ill nature also adds that only the hand could have been painted by Raphael; even so it is more in the style of the Venetian school than any hand in any of the paintings known to be by Raphael. This hand is painted more quickly, with more warmth; it aims more at the effect. Compare it with the hand of the handsome young man across the room, which I consider to be entirely by Raphael. The thrust of the arm bone in this Duke of Urbino's right hand is too near the little finger.

Nearby is an excellent copy of the *Madonna della Seggiola* by Monsieur Fabre. There are quite a number of his copies in this museum; and when he was not copying David and Talma, he was good. If one would fully appreciate Monsieur Fabre's talent, you must strain your eyes a little and look at number 65: "Tullius Driving His Chariot Over His Father's Body" by Dandré Bardon. That is what the French school had come to in 1780! Monarchic fastidiousness permitted no more than a third of the words in the language after the manner of the theater. If the monarchy had persisted in this effort, we would, I think, have ended up with Chinese politeness. A maker of paradoxes could maintain that because David was egotistical he loved freedom and all its excesses. We know that the people who adored Abbé Delille's verses did not like David's paintings.

Number 251. The Death of Saint Cecilia, a charming bas-relief by Poussin, is perhaps the best picture in the museum. We have seen in Rome the bath that was heated to excess for this pretty saint in the hope that she would be suffocated by the steam from the boiling water. She withstood that first test miraculously; then they decided to cut off her head. Though she received three blows of the sword they did not succeed in decapitating her, but she died later of her wounds. Who does not know the admirable and novel statue of Saint Cecilia in the convent of that name in the Transteverine? In its nuances of light and shade it is reminiscent of Raphael. Without any doubt this statue put Poussin on his mettle. Admirable tenseness of the saint's left thigh, a natural touch that is alone worth all of Poussin's paintings we have in Paris.

Saint Cecilia's figure has a length of ten heads. Holy women are soaking up her blood with sponges; a pope is blessing the dying saint. Two ridiculous acts which, in our opinion, dishonor the sublime death of this girl who, though so young and so beautiful, sacrificed her life to a belief.

There is much naturalness in Poussin's sketch (number 255), Rebecca giving Eliezer to drink, but the colors have reddened. It is in the manner of the *Noces Aldobrandines*, at that time much in fashion with scholars and pedants. You find those words harsh, I wager, but they would prefer them to Raphael.

Good portrait of Clement IX attributed to Poussin. Charming little angel's head by Baroche; they poisoned him, too, when he was quite young. He survived and later on painted several masterpieces, but he was always in poor health.

I admired three excellent landscapes by Boguet who lacked only the ability for intrigue to become the leading landscape painter in France. Boguet lived in Rome for sixty years; in fact he was a pupil, the best pupil, of Claude Lorrain. I criticize him for one thing only: the lights and shadows in his foregrounds are not strong enough.

Number 66. Beheading of Saint John by Daniel de Volterra. Very original painting; it is what one calls a new sidelight on such a "hackneyed" subject.

Number 92. By Van Dyck, a beautiful, very aristocratic hand clasping the hilt of a sword, remnant of a portrait destroyed by fire.

Number 106. Saint Mary, the Egyptian: horrible, old, all the more horrible as you see that she was once beautiful. The hands only are coarse and unnatural.

Number 139. Good Fra Bartolomeo, very pleasant, but is it really an original? Beside him, a charming little portrait of Alfieri.

Numbers 155, 156, 157. Excellent copies of Guaspré by Monsieur Fabre.

Number 167. Portrait of Petrarch attributed to Ghirlandaio. Face of a harsh pedant, a rich man; no trace of the author of the first sonnet.

Number 173. Torquato Tasso by Granet; Montaigne looks like a country priest, but Tasso is excellent.

Number 180. By Guercino, fine woman's head.

Number 188. Charming young girl looking at the sky, attributed to Guido Reni.

Number 215. Portrait of Cardinal, Duke of York, by Mengs. Quite the courteous and bewildered manner of a young prince mindful of the proprieties.

Number 238. Excellent view of a church vault lighted by torches; gives a fine idea of the vast size.

Number 242. The infant Jesus and the Virgin by Parmigianino. Charming, but perhaps a copy; hung too high to verify this point.

Number 274. Very curious portrait of Monsieur de Bâville, administrator and tyrant of Languedoc, as Saint-Simon calls him. Full face, aristocratic, stupid and dignified, like the face in the portrait of Racine. This portrait is hung fifteen feet high; it should be at eye level. It will be engraved for some future French edition of Tacitus.

Number 301. Pretty virgin by Il Sodoma. I pass over in silence a throng of mediocre paintings. This extremely pretty museum does not have any very reliable paintings by great masters; very inferior in that to the museum in Marseilles. I would give fifty estimable paintings from the Fabre Museum in exchange for Puget's *Saviour* and Ludovico Car- racci's *Assumption* (as full of defects as the latter is), which is in Mar- seilles. I shall not tell the city fathers of Montpellier that, for four thou- sand or five thousand francs, there are genuine Carracci to be found in Bologna.

Later on, I discovered two good portraits by a Montpellier artist— among others a distinguished old gentleman, wearing the cross of Saint Louis, who seems to be up in arms, if I may use that expression.

Number 338. Statue representing Summer, admirable in its absurd- ity. That, however, is what society adored in the days of Abbé Delille.

Number 342. Head of a Muse by Canova; charming face, but a trifle *bestiole*, as they say in Milan. Four horizontal folds at the neck which I could not approve of. Good portrait of genial Canova by Monsieur Fabre. But the marble pedestal is missing.

Fine landscape by Brascassat; cows and cattle in the style of Paul Potter, but with more warmth.

M . . . , a rich man from Paris, has left this museum many paint- ings from the Dutch school which I shall refrain from mentioning as I do not like them. To me it is the same as piano music compared to music for an orchestra. Admirable collection of sketches; a sketch by Raphael of a young man leaning in a window and looking down at the side. On this sketch I counted sixteen lines which appear to be in Ra- phael's handwriting and the rough copy of a poem, but the museum authorities have been clumsy enough, or prudent enough, to hang this sketch eight feet high. It should be on an eye level with the viewer. For that matter there is nothing easier than to make a mistake about Ra- phael's handwriting. I once happened on eighty letters or sonnets of Tasso. . . .

In the midst of all this display of provincial taste, the spirit is re- freshed by the sight of Italian paintings and by the foliage of a great tree that has not been trimmed.

# ·⸱⟨ Montpellier, *May 1, 1838* ⟩⸱·

The stupidity of these provincials is beyond belief. You may say what you please; but when you want to be materially comfortable, you must not leave the boulevards; anywhere else, you must look for only the sensations of the moment. You are always being surprised. For example, in Bayonne, I bought some sticks of that famous chocolate made especially for travelers. They are as thick and as long as your finger. But if you wanted to eat them on the journey, you would have to put the whole stick into your mouth, for the only way to break them is to pound them with a hammer.

Again this morning the wind was cold; as I was leaving I had the temerity to desire tea for breakfast. Taking some from the package M.C. had given me, I walked toward the best café in Montpellier, whose name I had finally learned to pronounce after several failures.

At the café I suffered the labors of Hercules to get some hot water, but with no success. In this cold weather I finally had to drink tea made of lukewarm water!

The Esplanade is illuminated; but the cold wind from the east has the same effect on me as the mistral, and spoils everything for me.

Montpellier must be counted among the ugly towns I have visited. It has an ugliness all its own in that it has no special character. The traveler is constantly going up and down hills. The streets are short and narrow and never twenty-five yards in a straight line. The houses are made of stone and are usually three stories high, but they are small, mean and lack distinction. There are no churches, only a ridiculous cathedral; but one of the most beautiful promenades in the world where, sooner or later, trees will be planted, for the trees at Peyrou are so few in number that they do not provide any shade.

Leave on May 3rd at eleven o'clock for Nîmes. To reach Arles must go by way of Nîmes.

*Marseilles: the Port*

# ⊸[ Marseilles, *May 7, 1838* [31] ]⊶

Yesterday, Sunday, at nine o'clock at night, I arrived from Martigues, extremely tired. This morning I strolled happily around this pretty town.

The doors of the houses remind me of London. They are small, made of pretty polished wood and equipped with locks and small, but very shiny, brass knockers. To enter you go up two steps from the pavement which is separated from the street by a little stream of clear water flowing very swiftly, for all the streets are sloping. It is understood, of course, that I am speaking only of the new city; as I have already said, one goes into the old town only to hide.

If Bordeaux is the most beautiful city in France, Marseilles is the prettiest. This quality it owes to certain avenues of plane trees, planted at the bottom of a very wide-mouthed valley which starts in the center of the town and rises gradually. It is a continuation of the harbor; and while enjoying the fresh air and the shade beneath plane trees sixty feet high and two feet in circumference, you can see the masts of vessels and the façades of the Fort Saint-Nicholas. I confess that, on a fine sunny day, there is no sight comparable to the Allées de Meilhan.

At the top of the avenue are four rows of enormously high old elms. The paved walks in that part of the city run the full length of the houses. From this point, avenues of plane trees stretch out into the countryside toward Saint-Just and the Madeleine, but it was too hot for me to follow them to the end.

I visited the church of Saint-Vincent-de-Paul, modern and very commonplace. With the gaiety of those avenues of plane trees and the proud, Greek features of the people of Marseilles, there should be an ancient temple here or at least one of those churches built in the manner of Palladio like San Fedele in Milan or San Nicola di Tolentino in Rome.

Rue Noailles which runs from the Cours Saint-Louis to the Allées de

[31] From May 6th to the 29th, sojourn one may call charming except for the rain during the first days. Arrived May 6th, but managed to tear myself away on the 29th after twenty-three days, seven or eight of which I spent in Grasse, Cannes and Fréjus. On the 29th went to Saint-Rémy by "the monument"; from there to Tarascon and tomorrow to Beaucaire.

*Marseilles: Mouth of the Rhone*

Meilhan, though fairly narrow, has two pavements and two streams, but every other moment the passer-by is forced to regulate his step to the steps of the persons in front of him. This congestion reminded me of Paris and the rue Vivienne. Marseilles also has cabs that could run you over, omnibuses, etc., but the pavement is never wet and the two streams always flow swiftly on both sides of the street.

Many houses have little gardens in which there are great numbers of big trees, or at least they allow us a glimpse of those gardens. It is all quite simple. This city was not built haphazardly by private interests, but was laid out by men of good sense around the year 1780. The blocks of houses are shaped like playing cards or like a square and the center has been left as a garden.

In warm weather the street door is left half open which creates a delightful draft with the garden and, at the same time, keeps the house dark. This, as you can see, is all one could possibly desire. Moreover people live for the most part on the ground floor; the windows have bars that jut out over the street so that one can sit in the space behind them. In a word, material life, as far as bodily comfort is concerned, is the direct opposite of life in Paris. Men spend their lives at their clubs and many of those clubs have gardens.

If the reader is in Marseilles, he will find that I cannot say enough good about this climate and the physical conditions of life here; but if the wind from the northwest (the mistral) blows, he will curse Marseilles and think only of leaving it. In that case one washes one's hands and face with oil of sweet almonds.

*Marseilles: a General View*

*Marseilles: a General View*

## ⋯⊲[ Marseilles, *May 9* ]⊳⋯

### *La Tourette and la Major*

If I lived in Marseilles I would flout fashion, which does not play an important part in this land of nature, and I would find a house in La Tourette. It is a magnificent terrace, one hundred feet above the sea from which one is separated only by a natural precipice. No factories, no thought of utilities, nothing petty. Only an old, decaying wall between us and the deep sea.

This terrace of La Tourette, where I have just been drenched to the skin (having left my umbrella behind at the Hôtel du Nord in Arles), marks the end of the old town. It is subject to the most violent mistral (the wind from the northwest); but here we are only twenty minutes from the theater and the fashionable section of town, though the natural road to reach them is by way of the pretty quai de la Bourse, the liveliest and gayest in France.

This terrace of La Tourette was, I think, the center of the Marseilles Caesar beseiged. It is supposed that the sea carried off a great part of the soil of that ancient city. The old town in Marseilles, situated on the hill to the west of the harbor, is very large, but one never goes there. At every step, thanks to the prefect Thibaudeau (the historian) one finds boundary marks, fountains and little squares filled with leaves from three or four handsome plane trees. These trees, whose foliage is not very dense and therefore does not interfere with the view, are popular in Greece. They look especially well when ranged the full length of the houses.

The streets in this old town are narrow and, as they occupy the summit and the slopes of a small hill, you are always going uphill and down dale. There are some fine vistas, both toward Notre-Dame-de-la-Garde and toward the sea; but while the streets are uglier than the streets in the interior of Montpellier, I like them much better because of the views. The view from the third floor of the houses must be delightful.

As in Naples here, too, the inhabitants live on the street. Though they obligingly showed me the way to la Major, they had difficulty in understanding me. You have to say *Majour*, and all feminine words end

188

*Marseilles: from the Réserve*

*Marseilles: View of the Port*

in *o*. I can understand everything they say from my knowledge of Italian, but to speak their language is a different matter.

La Major (the cathedral), which I finally reached and which scholars have established on the ruins of a temple of Diana, like the church in Ancona (is it Diana in Ancona?), is only a poor village church not worth describing. An organ fills the entrance, which is through the second chapel on the right. I found a nave and two aisles, several semicircular arches and a number of pillars whose cross section ended, on all sides, in right angles—therefore a Romanesque church, but of the poorest type.[32]

The only Gothic architecture I found was in a very small chapel lighted by a dome at the rear on the left. On the left in that chapel with its Gothic vaulted ribs was a large bas-relief of Jesus in the tomb, the figures life-size and raised. The front of the altar is also a bas-relief which is part of a tomb, the Virgin and two saints beneath three porticoes formed by short columns. Architects were still copying Greco-Roman forms in those days.

On the other hand two arcades in the little Gothic chapel against the left wall of the church are in the Renaissance style. The detached column and the two pillars that form the three arcades are adorned with little angels, stalks of wheat, plants and other embellishments, all rather poorly carved but belonging to the delicate genre of the Florentine school, like those decorations one admires on the tomb of Francis I at Saint-Denis.

Beneath those arches there is an altar and two little structures shaped like an armoire, one of them terminating in a triangular frontispiece surmounted by a cupola. On it I read the date MIIIICLXXXI (1481); the other ends in a semicircular frontispiece. It is all rather poorly done. The altar reminded me of the charming little cupids Raphael painted in his youth. It has a marble armoire divided into seven compartments; there are some carved bas-reliefs like the bas-reliefs of children one sees along walls, but very clear and which, in that place, should greatly impress people who are not shocked by the absence of form. Those bas-reliefs depict, it seems to me, the story of Saint Lazarus who, after having been raised from the dead by Jesus, came to Marseilles to found this church. The figures are not very raised.

[32] Must verify this. See *Gallia Christiana* and *Academus*.

There was a strong odor in this church. A poor priest was teaching some wretched children the catechism, the article of confession, and doing his best to restrain the impatience his voice betrayed. On the other hand, the children simply could not understand that it is a sacrilege not to confess all one's sins. In spite of the smell, I lingered there a long time, listening and imagining that same patience applied to explaining the sin of *stealing* to these children, every single one of whom knew perfectly well what stealing was.

On the right of what must be the main door of la Major, in the corner of the wall, I noticed a little hexagonal structure perhaps eight feet in diameter whose cupola was supported by two little fluted Corinthian columns. The altar is formed by the front of an ancient tomb: on the ends, two upright figures; then, flattened and vertical SS; in the middle, three figures whose heads seem to me rather poorly carved. Because it was raining, the church was very dark (Milin atlas, Plate 59, diagram 4). There is a Roman magistrate near him with some manuscripts held together by a strap.

For that matter everyone has robbed this poor la Major church. Henri IV had some of the beautiful columns removed. Count de Tende took two columns from la Major and sent them to his brother-in-law, the High Constable de Montmorency. In the circular space around the high altar I saw three large paintings, poor but very clear, very intelligible. At one time there were some of Puget's paintings here, but they have since been hung in the museum.

At the high altar they have left a large slab of marble, sculptured and divided into three arches; the Madonna and the infant Jesus occupy the one in the middle. The others are occupied by saints bearing the stole, a low mitre, and a large cross with the head of a snake on the top.

The stock exchange is at the harbor in an excellent position facing south. It is on a square that juts out into the harbor and, across from it stands the rock of Notre-Dame-de-la-Garde, which seems to be placed there expressly for the view. On that pointed rock there is not a single tree, only a few missionaries' crosses and, at the top, the fort built by Francis I.

Behind the stock exchange is the town hall, which is connected with the exchange by an archway over the street. It looked to me as though

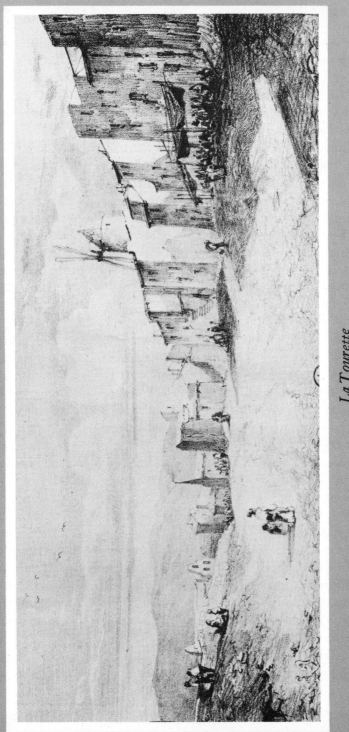

*La Tourette*

there was only one staircase for the two buildings and this staircase, where the statue of Libertat stands, is in the town hall. These two buildings, which are really one, are reached by that pretty quay paved with bricks set edgewise (the *opus spicatum* of the ancients), whose gaiety and naturalness I have so often praised. All the merchants in town come to this quay at four o'clock.

The façade is one main building, flanked by two pavilions. The peculiar thing about it is that on the first floor the main building is set back from the pavilions; but, in compensation, on the ground floor, the middle part projects. This middle section has three windows, the one in the center being the lowest, and the pavilions have two windows each.

The balcony is supported by rather pretty columns for which niches have been made and in which they are half hidden. The façade and even the sides of the building are so covered with ornamentation that there is no smooth surface left on which to express its own language. But all that is not too ugly.

Part of the fine effect is due to the position of this building which is flanked, at only a short distance, by a vast number of ships' masts. In front of it a beautiful square leads to the harbor and beyond it and directly opposite rises the arid mountain of Notre-Dame-de-la-Garde crowned by the fort built by Francis I, its pointed contours outlined against the sky. From the stock exchange, the port of Marseilles looks like a lake filled with ships. You cannot see the sea.

A new bust has been set up in the center of the façade at such a ridiculous height that I could not see whether it was a bust of Louis XIV or of the reigning king who, for that matter, looks very much like his ancestor.

Do not look for anything like the character of the Marseillais in all France. And that is what charms me about this part of the country. The Marseillais is frank, even coarse; he says what he thinks even when that happens to be contrary to politeness. In other places people listen to long stories, but a man from Marseilles makes two or three little gestures, then says to the tiresome fellow who is boring him: "Pardon me, sir, I haven't time today," and off he goes. In his business affairs the Marseillais is scrupulously honest.

Working in Marseilles is not like working in Paris, Rouen, and even less, in Lyons. Here the businessman goes to the Casati stock exchange

*Marseilles: View of Notre-Dame-de-la-Garde*

(it is the Tortoni of this part of the world) at ten o'clock in the morning. In the afternoon at four o'clock he goes to the actual stock exchange on the harbor; but for the rest, he is almost never in his office. As for Sundays, nothing on earth would make him sacrifice his day in the country at his shooting box. One day my friend N. decided to risk one hundred fifty *louis* on an experiment. He arranged to meet a merchant we both know on Sunday at seven o'clock in the morning. He offered the merchant an excellent business deal on a certain commodity on which he stood to earn 5 per cent, probably without having to move it. The Marseillais quickly got the point: he would have to stay in town forty or fifty minutes longer to inspect the merchandise. For fifteen or twenty minutes he tried his best to lure N. with him to his shooting box and so well did he plead that we witnesses feared the bet was lost. But finding that N. would not budge, he finally exclaimed: "Business tomorrow!" and, putting the old nag harnessed to his cabriolet to a gallop, off he dashed at top speed.

There is a vast difference between the character of the man from Marseilles and the character of the man from Lyons and an even greater difference, though in another sense, from the Parisian's character. Monsieur de Villèle[33] once told one of his clerks that the quality a man in his position needed most was the ability to learn to be bored. Two days later, when the clerk went in to hand Monsieur de Villèle some work he had done on a matter de Villèle had to defend in court that same day, the clerk found him, at seven o'clock in the morning, listening to advice from S. de L. With great difficulty the clever minister extricated himself from this boring situation and, turning to his clerk, said simply: "You see."

The Marseillais is absolutely incapable of exercising the Parisian's first qualification for success in life: knowing how to be bored and even more, if possible, the second qualification: never to hurt anyone.

When he talks about a merchant he knows, the Marseillais will give you a complete résumé in a nutshell: the amount of money the man has; his method of doing business; how intelligent he is; his social status and, if he is married, his wife's life story.

As far as the material side of civilization is concerned, Marseilles

[33] Joseph, Count de Villèle (1773–1854): French statesman born in Toulouse and leader of the ultra-royalists under the Restoration. (Translator's note)

ranks obviously as the second city in France. When I arrived here last night, tired out, exhausted, I longed for a cup of tea so I went to the Café des Milles Colonnes, where the setting and décor would do credit to Paris. "Will it be possible to get any hot water?" I wondered.

I was served a tea so hot it scalded me and, as to the quality, it was the average tea one expects in a café. In Lyons, I would have resisted this desire, for God knows what I would have found in those Lyons cafés at half-past nine on a Sunday night! The waiter would have given me a surly reply as though I had made an importunate request and would have brought me heaven only knows what sort of lukewarm concoction. In Bordeaux, I would have taken a chance, not however in the Café Montesquieu where I would have had to repeat my order three or four times; but in the Café de la Comédie where, after a delay of twenty minutes, I would have been politely served—cold tea. In Marseilles I was served in two minutes and with marked deference.

"Monsieur, just wait a little if you want the tea to be properly made." It is true the waiter did not say: "I advise Monsieur to wait a little, if he wishes etc. . . ."

The café where I had breakfast this morning (tea, cream, rolls and butter) was very crowded, with the result that out of perhaps fifty tables only one was vacant. Seeing that I did not have a newspaper or a cigar, the owner came over to ask if I were being kept waiting. I replied with a compliment to which he did not pay much attention. But this man is very good at making the waiters step around. How different from the waiter at the Hôtel du Nord the day before yesterday at Arles! This, in my opinion, is one of the greatest pleasures of traveling.

Arles is a hole which the traveler visits only for its admirable antiquities. I was alone in the dining room when I talked to the Arlesian waiter. In the Marseilles café there were one hundred and fifty people all talking loudly, the majority asking for something. In addition there was an abominable singer, unattractive and singing off key on all the notes above high E. In the middle of this appalling din, the polite waiter took my order quickly and the owner, seeing that I was waiting, came over to ask me what I had ordered.

The reader will perhaps have noticed my habit of measuring the degree of civilization by the degree of hot water I am served. My answer is that I believe only what I see and these little details are very important.

At the café I found three or four of my broker friends: young men from twenty-five to thirty years old, very well dressed, who earn five thousand to eight thousand francs by walking around from nine until four o'clock with some samples and a lot of cigars in their pockets. To work all a man need do is to come out of his house. Most business is done in the cafés. Men meet each other in the café and they talk business as they stroll about the streets in the shade. A good life indeed! As I had not been in Marseilles for two years, each of my friends gave me three or four thumbnail sketches of acquaintances to whom something good or bad had happened in the interval. All these biographies were spicy and highly imprudent.

To add to my pleasure this morning, I was actually too warm while walking in the shade and I was delighted to find a little breeze on the Cannebière (rue du Chanvre, built fifty years ago on land where hemp had been grown). This is the principal street in Marseilles. It is broader than the rue de la Paix (in Paris) and leads from the Cours to the harbor which can be seen at that point in all its breadth. All the streets east and south of the Cannebière are perfectly straight and have pavements on both sides. The old town lies north and west of the Cannebière. No respectable man ever goes into the old town, though he can have a flat there if he happens to be in love. Love is, I think, a rare weakness in Marseilles. Here ladies in good society do not let themselves be kidnapped as they do in Bordeaux to go and live with their lover in a fifth-floor apartment in Paris. In Marseilles a man falls in love only with those persons who are rather difficult to mention in a book: I shall therefore say only with young girls of easy virtue.

While we were having dinner, one of my friends told me that last year he had made up his mind to go to Paris, enjoy its pleasures and spend six months there that were to be a high point in his life.

"I was bored in your Paris," he said, "and I prefer a thousand times my shooting box where I hunt Sunday mornings to all the groves in Sceaux and Verrières." And he went on to enumerate the long list of his preferences. Notice that at this shooting box in the country there are often not even as many as four green trees. The poorest and most scraggly tree on the boulevards would arouse public admiration in one

*Marseilles: Café-Restaurant*

*Marseilles: Cannebiére*

of those shooting boxes of which there are five or six thousand in the
environs of Marseilles. On all sides one sees these little dazzlingly white
houses standing out against the sickly green of olive trees.

## The Museum

Marseilles is like Rome in that it is built on several hills, but would to
heaven that Rome could have a view of the sea at the foot of one of its
hills! On one of Marseilles' hills, which is reached by a beautiful avenue
of plane trees, stands the convent of the Bernardins and it is the church
of that convent that has been turned into a museum.

This Marseilles museum is impressive in its dimness. It is built in the
shape of a capital T with only the branches of the T feebly lit so that,
toward the point where the two lines meet, there is total darkness. And
it is precisely at that point that the city fathers have chosen to hang
Rubens' *The Boar Hunt*, a magnificent painting, because the subject is
exactly suited to the great artist's blaze of colors and extravagant de-
sign.

A tree trunk, painted bluish and so false that one does not know at
first what it is, lies across the painting horizontally at the base. Above it
is a boar. A man, half naked, frightened, is thrusting a spear at the boar
which is not looking at him. Like all the other living figures in the
painting, except the dogs, the boar (magnificently painted for that matter) is cool and collected. He is looking at another man who calmly
thrusts a hunting spear into the animal's jaw.

A stout burgomaster on horseback appears beyond the boar and
deliberately touches the top of the boar's head with his sword. Only
the dogs are admirable. They are indeed above all praise. Several of
them are covered with blood, which is probably why they are taking
the situation very seriously. There are six dogs, nine human beings and
two horses. From the little one sees of the leaves on the trees, they are
blue. Two rather pretty women stand three feet away from the boar,
gazing at him with the most perfect sang-froid. This painting seems to
me to have been hastily improvised; the boar's back is not even finished. Hakkert, in Naples, finishes his boars quite differently, but where
is the divine fire?

*The Assumption* by Ludovico Carracci makes all the paintings near it appear insignificant; this is almost its only merit. The head of the Madonna is commonplace, her gesture as she flings out her arms violently is exaggerated. The strength of the chiaroscura and the freedom of the gestures mark this painting as first-class. Admirable details: little angels, probably of the Venetian school; the larger angels are boys of eighteen. The feet of the angel on the right attract too much attention and lack grace, but not verity.

Shocked by the affectation and falsity of the conventional with which the fools who styled themselves successors of Raphael filled their paintings, the Carracci had the courage to revert to truth. That idea and the superhuman courage with which they pursued it (see their historian, Malvasio) almost brought them to the verge of starvation. As a model for the angel, Ludovico Carracci chose a handsome eighteen-year-old boy and would not have dreamed of giving him a woman's feet to add to the appearance of holiness. The Carracci had too great a horror and scorn of any falseness.

In the darkest corner of the museum hangs one of Raphael's paintings: *Saint John Writing the Apocalypse.* To tell the truth, this time I think the city fathers, those all-powerful directors of the museum, were being spiteful. If this painting is by Raphael, it is far and away the poorest one left us by this great artist. Everyone knows his talent for portraying the slightest nuances of passion with a brilliance and especially a depth that never detracts from perfect truth. In particular he excels in depicting respect, devoutness, sublime devotion. But this Saint John sits astride an eagle like a dolt; he looks as though he is dreaming of other things as he listens to divine inspiration. His attitude is more than foolish; it is stupid. Moreover there is a slight anachronism: to write on a stone tablet he is about to use a pen. The Paris museum sent this painting to the people of Marseilles at the time their museum was opened. Those who claim that it is an original say it was part of a former collection of the king's and that it had been engraved by Simonneau. One would have to see it at close quarters in broad daylight and examine it through a magnifying glass. I would say it is a copy made in the artist's day but by a pupil who did not know how to see or at least to reproduce the nuances of expression which, in the painting attributed to Raphael, compensated for the awkward position of arms and legs. Far from being inspired like the head by Domenichino, of the same Saint John also writing his gospel in Saint Andrea delle Frate in Rome, this head is ridiculous; as for the painting, the bare arms and legs are particularly bad. In fact I do not see any good painting in the whole picture except in the eagle's talons and the fingers of the left hand.

All that being granted, I am far from believing that Raphael never did anything that was mediocre. But if we look closely at his less perfect figures, the mind rejects so violently things that would mortally offend us in a mediocre painter, that even his slightest works make a tremendous impression. Try as we may, we cannot shut our eyes to the fact that, as the result of our disillusionment in looking at mediocre paintings, we form the habit of practically ignoring any paintings not signed by a great name.

This Marseilles museum cannot compete with the Montpellier museum in the number of paintings a trifle above the mediocre that charm and captivate the vulgar herd, but in actual fact it is far superior to it. It has a painting by Giulio Romano of three horsemen mounted on heavy cart horses; the horse on the right and the young rider are above all praise. They also have *The Farewells of Priam and Hector*, by Guercino, a night scene by torch light. Priam's dressing gown is admirable. This museum has the list of Guercino's paintings in his own handwriting. It is obvious that he often painted only to earn money; this painting did not make him dream for even half an hour. He was given the order and immediately set to work to paint an old man in a dressing gown and a tall young man garbed as a Roman warrior. Neither of them is moved in the least; but such as this painting is, no good modern painter (I mean one born since the death of Poussin) could have done anything to compare with it.

There is an excellent Caravaggio here, but very unimportant: a corpse supported by two twelve-year-old children. It is called: *The dead Jesus Christ supported by two angels*. I noticed a good copy of Domenichino's *The Penitent Magdalen*, which the catalogue says is an original, and perhaps it is an original ruined by the sun. At one time the court of Naples inherited some Correggios that had belonged to the Farnese. For ten years those paintings lay at the foot of a staircase, turned against a wall and every passer-by p. . . . on them. This poor little Domenichino may have met the same fate. In Naples, even in our day, one sees how the sun scorches the magnificent Canalettos. On the other hand there can be no doubt as to the originality of the Father Eternal and the fine head of Lanfranco, that intriguer who poisoned the good Domenichino's life.

This museum owns a magnificent Perugino in which Saint Anne appears above the Madonna who is seated on a throne at an altar. The absence of thought, which distinguishes Perugino, is here concealed by the number of human figures and their profound and reverent timidity. The name of each saint is inscribed in his halo. Below the Virgin's throne the artist has signed his name in letters that are much too large. The flesh tints verge on pale yellow, the result of time. This painting, in which every leaf on a tree is plainly visible, is more than three centuries old.

The general tone in this master's painting is gold. The sun sets through an orange cloud. Here the color has faded, the flesh tints and the highlights verge on pale yellow. Perugino was probably jealous of his pupil Raphael's tremendous success. Today he owes three-quarters of his own fame to that pupil alone. And Raphael could never completely rid himself of the pettiness learned in the school of Perugino. Fra Bartolomeo, who gave him chiaroscura, could not give him the *bold style.*

One cannot praise the same clarity in an excellent landscape by Annibale Carracci. It is a hasty imitation of the sublime landscapes he had seen in Venice, of which the finest example is the glory of Camuccini's gallery in Rome (next to the Palazzo Borghese). This handsome painting by Annibale Carracci should be washed with lukewarm water; the sight of it would be very useful to those provincial landscapists who are so finicky and so lacking in a noble style.

I saw a pretty guardian angel by Feti, of which no doubt the hard pressed engravers, who print books of hours, have never heard. Opposite it is a commonplace Madonna by Maratta, that extraordinarily vulgar painter.

The paintings the government sends to museums in the provinces are incredible. In Toulouse I was struck by Langlois' *Apelle et Campaspe*, because the daily newspaper announced that the artist had just been made a member of the Institute. Here one finds Dufau's *Gustave Vasa haranguant les Dalécarliens,* Duvivier's *Cymodocée,* Mallet's *La Nature et l'Honneur,* and in particular the *Blessing of the Flocks* by

Mongin, etc. In my opinion a minister who perpetrates a crime like that deserves to be committed for trial. But those gentlemen even dare to talk art and one is obliged to listen to them with a straight face!

Here, however, more than the minister is involved! The mayor of Marseilles, the Marquis de Montpaon, took it upon himself to acquire paintings for the museum instead of spending two thousand francs to have a large window opened at the point where the two lines of the capital T meet. They took the nave and the crosspieces from a church. The nave has four columns on each side, but they should have left the skylight in the dome or at least have cut in an immense window. I can see two or three ways it could have been done, but it would take too long to explain here. The Marquis de Montpaon bought *Noah's First Sacrifice on Leaving the Ark*, *View of la Cava near Naples*, *Marcus Curius receiving the Deputies from Pyrrhus*. Judging from this choice, I should say that the worthy mayor should have been appointed Minister of the Interior.

The holy rage in which those official paintings put me was dissipated by a charming copy of Poussin's *Flora*, the original of which, eaten away and damaged by time, is in the Capitoline museum in Rome. The copyist has captured and reproduced the grace of the nymph gathering a flower in the foreground. However, that good man, it must be added, has no nobility of style. He paints rapidly like Joseph Vernet, but his figures are bright, intelligible and show us Poussin's figures just as they emerged from the studio. That is an excellent commentary on this great artist's painting.

I noticed a head, said to be a portrait of the celebrated Racine, which is quite as pleasing as the alleged portrait of Racine in the Toulouse museum. The Racine in Toulouse is a wily magistrate with the face of a fox; the one in Marseilles is a satisfied prig. The editor of the museum's guidebook could not have had enough curiosity to look at the engraving of the great and imposing, but foolish, figure of Louis XIV's poet. The satisfied prig in Marseilles is resting one arm on a large book on the back of which one can read the words: Corn. Tacitus.

I pass over in silence many interesting paintings, for example *Mercure* from the Farnesina, copied by Ingres—who has made Raphael's forms a trifle heavy—and *Savior of the World*, a very remarkable painting by Puget (born in Marseilles in 1662, painter, architect and sculptor). The head of the Savior is too large, but the angels are painted in the grand manner. I do not know whether Poussin himself has anything better. This man is an artist of the first order. I have seen this picture only five or six times; nevertheless I would venture to say that what distinguishes Puget as a painter is his distribution of light.

Among painters I would place Puget immediately after Poussin and Le Sueur. I would add that Le Sueur is superior to him only in ideas; he never painted angels comparable to the angels in this picture. My advice to a Minister of the Interior with an appreciation of art would be: "Send Marseilles a fine Domenichino—beauty of color is important to people in the provinces—and hang a painting by Puget in Paris."

I was surprised to see twenty-four paintings by Michel Serre, an unknown artist, born in Catalonia in 1658, who died in Marseilles in 1733. He was extremely poor and knew how to be sparing with light. I consider him far superior to all the other mediocre painters who fill the bays of the French school in the Musée de Paris.

Serre showed astonishing courage during the plague in Marseilles in 1720; but his pictures, painted with colors and on canvas bought at a discount, have darkened, and the Marseilles museum is ridiculously dim. I noticed a head by Serre in imitation of Correggio in his *Presentation at the Temple*. These paintings by Serre should be spread around in all the museums in France. His defects are not French defects (no relief, false color, figures copied from the artist then in fashion). I was pleased to see two paintings, very faded it is true, by Le Sueur. Nor must we omit two immense canvases by Vien which seem miraculous compared to the *Christ On The Cross* by Dandré Bardon, or to *The Fourth Act of Iphigenia in Aulis* by Monsiau, a painting ordered by the Minister of the Interior. We must also mention another gift from the government: *Ulysses acknowledged by Eurycleia* painted by Tardieu.

The strange thing about these museums in the provinces are the portraits. I still remember Descartes, Henry de Montmorency and Cinq-Mars in Toulouse. Here I found an excellent Madame de Pompadour in the blue painting of the era, and the portrait of Lord Staffard, shown apparently at the moment when he learned that his friend, King Charles I, had signed his death warrant. I wish the portrait might be considered a good likeness. The guidebook attributes it to Van Dyck, which is

*Marseilles: the Cours*

absurd. In this portrait Lord Staffard looks like a man from the South of France, a big drummer from Nîmes, without any finesse or nobility, but he is energetic and his expression is full of deep melancholy.

The portrait of Madame de Pompadour, in the guise of Aurora, so the guidebook says, is by Nattier. The museum also has a *Christ battu* by Rubens (number 130), a mass of very ignoble and very red flesh. Enormous dullness of style and above all no divine afflatus in the God-man.

A very curious, very unusual, painting by Rubens is the *Family of the Prince of Orange*. The prince is ridiculous, both in figure and in his expression. He is dressed in the heroic style of the Louis XIV at the Porte Saint-Denis. His knee is bare and that knee is crippled. But the children's heads are very good; not quite so good, however, is the head of the princess, whose ugliness cannot be blamed on the artist who, no doubt, lied as much as he could.

This large painting is surrounded by thirty-eight medallions in grisaille, dark-brown in color. Most of the round medallions have two heads and bear inscriptions. This picture is hung too high.

"It is the gifts from the Minister of the Interior," I would say to the city fathers, "that should be hung at this height."

For that matter everything here is arranged contrary to common sense. Raphael should have been placed where *Hercules Between Vice and Virtue,* that mawkish insipidity attributed to Crayer, hangs. Rubens' *The Boar Hunt* should have been hung where the *Glorification of Mary Magdalen* now hangs and, facing it or at the side, Guerclain's *Priam,* Domenichino's *Mary Magdalen Repentant* and Annibale Carracci's *Landscape*.

I don't know what the editor of the Marseilles' guidebook had against Philippe de Champaigne for him to have attributed to Champaigne an *Assumption of the Holy Virgin,* a blue painting worth all the Restouts in the world. Philippe de Champaigne is yellow and pious. A *Glorification of Mary Magdalen,* attributed to him, looked to me like a copy of some good painting.

As a result of his hatred for the name of Champaigne, the editor of the guidebook attributes to Jean-Baptiste, a pupil of Philippe's, a *Stoning of Saint Paul,* the chef d'oeuvre of some poor pupil of David.

There is a *Dying Mary Magdalen* by Finsonius, which is not bad.

Twenty or thirty pictures in this museum deserve the same praise—for example, a madonna in the manner of Sassoferrato (number 177), a portrait by Drouais, another (a weasel-faced woman, number 12) by Fauchier d'Aix, a storm by Henry d'Arles. Puget, the son of the great artist, painted a *Visitation* in which the figures look like actors.

This museum has two immense paintings by Vien; they are cold but not affected and could almost pass for chefs d'oeuvre after one has seen the paintings of Messrs. Dandré Bardon, Restout, Van Loo, Coypel and de Troy. There is a *Visitation* by Geminiani of Genoa, not bad; a *Roman Charity*, inaccurately attributed to Guido Reni, *idem*. By Raoux there is a *Young Girl Writing to Her Lover;* her grandmother is reading over her shoulder. This picture must have had a great success in 1730; an ingenuous painter (if there is such a creature) ought to copy it and switch the heads.

For a long time I stood motionless before Puget's bust. It is not like those busts of great painters that spoil the Musée de Paris. This bust, which looks to me like a conscientious copy, deserves the full attention of all lovers of art. It is completely naturalistic like all of his works. A square head, the tight-lipped mouth of a man who is making a great effort to control himself, eyes irregular, the right eye much lower than the left—in general, many characteristics scrupulously, that is, precisely, reproduced the way finicky portraitists copy every wart.

Behind Puget's bust is a little *Assumption* by him, three feet high: the Madonna, a few clouds and two angels. Admirable simplicity, exquisite naturalness of the Virgin's head and her gesture. I could see only one defect in it: this figure has a total height of ten heads.

Toulon had the good sense to have the two famous terminals that support the balcony of its city hall molded in plaster and to send a copy to Marseilles where they have been placed on either side of the inner door of the museum.

In 1656 Puget carved them out of stone from Calissano, a work that made the great man's reputation. Their defects today are probably the very thing that made their originality pardoned in 1656. I am speaking of that exuberance of flowering garlands, of baroque shells and other ornaments from beneath which emerge those poor devils condemned to hold up the balcony. This is certainly a case of girding oneself with flowers! Their faces clearly show their anguish.

These caryatids under balconies were the fashion in Marseilles a century ago—the result of its proximity to Italy and especially to Genoa. If instead of appearing in 1656, at the age of thirty-four, before a public which still had the vigor of the Fronde, poor Puget had not made his début until 1680—after Racine—he would have been even more scorned than he was. The magistrates of Toulon had quoted him a price of one thousand five hundred francs for the statue. Puget pointed out modestly that the block of marble alone cost him. . . .

In Marseilles, that very Greek city, so ancient, so important and so rich under the emperors, there is not a marble of any real value. No other museum would want any of the marbles the Marseilles museum has collected. If Marseilles had been destroyed by an earthquake, what phrases bombastic authors would have written on the "magnificent" monuments the earthquake had robbed posterity of! Arles and Fréjus have a hundred times more antiquities than Marseilles.

Marseilles has increased in size, has undergone a change and has become richer, perhaps more powerful. It has built its new houses from the debris of ancient buildings. Arles and Fréjus, once fairly large cities, have been reduced to a third of their size and any ancient monuments they may have are still to be discovered.

And now, to hold the attention of the reader who may still be lingering in the lobby of this museum, let me say a few words about those unfortunate marbles.

Number 5. A seated woman holds out her right hand to a man who is standing. The gesture implies confidence and intimacy. We see from what is left of the center of the bas-relief that, between the two figures, there was a woman carrying a babe in swaddling clothes. The figure of the babe is complete, his head covered with a cap. To what national costume does this cap belong? What is left of this bas-relief is mediocre, but the artist had been trained in a good school. Thus a fool in 1838 writes better than a semi-talented man in 1738; it is not that the school is any better, but instruction is more widely spread. The work on this bas-relief is said to be Greek; I would not think so, but then I have not examined it long enough to form an opinion.

Number 11. Tomb of Glaucias discovered in 1799 beneath the ruins of the Abbey of Saint Victor. On the tomb one can read clearly a Greek inscription of seven rather dull lines. The son of Glaucias, speaking to his father, says: "Thy son would have given thee not a tomb, but sustenance and solace in thine old age." Moral sentiments have made tremendous progress since the days of the Greeks: we no longer boast of giving food to our fathers. It is this progress which makes all the books in Greek prose a trifle foolish. Scholars, naïve by profession, and often paid to lie, are not aware of this misfortune or at least they take good care to come to terms with it.

Number 13 is perhaps the best marble in this museum. It is a tomb eight feet long by three and one half feet high (note 32): centaurs are fighting some lions at whom they are hurling rocks. The heads are worn. This monument of better days was found in Arles. The inscription bears the name of Flavius Memorius who, no doubt, took possession of this tomb built for a dead man from a better era than his.

Numbers 14 to 21 are Christian tombs.

Number 27. Some rather mediocre engineers are forging weapons. Two of them hold up a medallion on which one sees the she-wolf, Romulus and Remus. Above this escutcheon is a sphinx.

Number 28. Several centaurs surround a medallion held aloft by two Victories. On it one reads: IULIÆ QUINTINÆ. This pagan tomb was used at the beginning of the ninth century for Saint Mauront, bishop of Marseilles.

One of the exhibits is a basalt figure of an Egyptian woman. A sort of polygonal rose is traced on the tip of her breasts, at the extremity of those natural charms so agreeable to the touch.

Against my firm resolve I have written at some length about this museum. It is incomparably the best as far as painting is concerned. The clear skies, the beautiful weather we have been having for the past eight days make one more receptive to the masterpieces of art. What a good effect these pictures would make if they were hung in a fine building like the museum in Toulouse or even a decent one like Arles. In those cities they have also used a church, but it never occurred to the authorities to top it with a second story and to block out all light from a museum. A novel idea to say the least! And this was done by an administration that buys pictures!

At Toulouse, at Arles, at Grenoble, they have put their museums in a church, but they were not so niggardly as they were in Marseilles as to give it only half the church (and the poorer half at that) and no daylight. A device worthy of a big city magistrate who goes to the town hall after dinner.

Speaking of the Maison Carrée in Nîmes, a magistrate said: "Let's tear this building down. We'll have a fine square and people won't always be coming to ask us for money" (historic). In 1838 Nîmes had perhaps fifty or one hundred francs for its museum which was housed in the Maison Carrée. Moreover it was in a pretty fix! Three-quarters of the pictures were turned against the wall and piles of paintings were covered with dust inches thick.

Two steps from this museum there is a very nice poultry market which is not yet finished. There are some columns backed against the wall: stones cut to resemble wreaths—very ridiculous. Attached columns would not have cost any more; but perhaps the building committee in Paris objected, just as they objected to having columns on the law court in Bourges. Peering through the boards over the market I saw on the steps a good statue of a prominent citizen seated and crowned with a wreath. Where the devil did they find him?

# ·◦❯ Marseilles, *May 10, 1838* [34] ❮◦·

## Commerce

And now I ask your permission to talk about business. The ease with which business is conducted in Marseilles always astonishes me. And after Marseilles, Nantes comes second. The most close-fisted, if I may be permitted to use this expression, are Bordeaux and especially Le Havre. My explanation of the difference is as follows: in Marseilles everyone makes his capital work for him. Most of the businessmen have eighty thousand *écus* and, by using their credit, do business for one hundred thousand *écus*.

In Le Havre young men, with nothing but talent and the need for a certain amount of luxury, do business with money furnished by a silent partner. They must: (1) serve the interests of the silent partners, and (2) provide luxury for Madame (if the young businessman is married). In Marseilles Madame knows how to cook, supervises their one maid who prepares the meals, if need be she cooks half the dinner herself. The domestic life in those households could not be simpler. In our opinion that is very respectable. A lady from Marseilles who has the keenest wit (everyone, even in Paris, would agree if I were to mention her name) entertained me greatly the other day with a dissertation on chick-peas. She was arguing with a Spaniard whose patriotism would not tolerate a joke about chick-peas.

Yesterday on the upper part of the rue Paradis I made a good deal by sending a present of wine to a correspondent from Genoa, excellent wine from Champagne with first-rate labels and all tied up and packed, ready to be shipped out. It cost me thirty sous the bottle.

Once in Genoa I attended a ball where all evening I heard our

---

[34] In 1838 we stayed in Marseilles at the Hôtel des Bouches-du-Rhone which was not rich enough to be indifferent to travelers. Dinner at Ducros, 19 rue Vacon. Coffee at the Milles-Colonnes, crowded, and at Bodoul, rue Saint-Ferréol, the clientele, upper middle class. Madame Camoin's reading room where profound silence reigns. This morning several Englishmen arrived and, true to their usual custom (to show their superiority by giving offense), began to talk loudly in high-pitched, affected voices. The English are an estimable nation, but extremely disagreeable. Everything displeases them. They want the whole world to be like England and they are constantly fleeing from that "home, sweet home" they praise so highly.

host's generosity praised to the skies all evening and where his lackeys did nothing but open bottles of wine from Champagne. I am convinced that my present made a great impression. So therefore I ordered some bottles of this same wine sent to a house where I had been invited to dine. But to be on the safe side I begged the mistress of the house not to give me away. No one criticized my wine. But in revenge, some Bordeaux wine, Saint-Julien, at twenty-five sous the bottle, was execrable and as thick as ink.

A house in Livorno, which does a tremendous business in oil with the North, sent to a friend in Petersburg . . .[35]

In Marseilles when you ask for information about a merchant, people never mention his fortune. They simply say: "he pays" or "he doesn't pay." And yet in this city they know every man's fortune down to the last penny. I was told yesterday that never has a banker in Marseilles gone bankrupt. ("Never" no doubt means "rarely.")

I needed money, but instead of getting it from a banker, on the 10th of the month I asked a merchant on whom I had a draft that fell due on the 30th, whether he would cash it for me.

"We'll talk it over at the stock exchange," he replied. "Come to such and such a number on the left-hand corner this afternoon."

I went there.

"I'll have it for you. Come back tomorrow morning."

"At what rate?"

"Three per cent."

I agreed. And people expect Marseilles not to resent it if the government refuses to redeem securities on which it pays 5 per cent!

If Algiers is not abandoned and if Marseilles keeps on at the rate it is going now (last month customs brought in two million two hundred thousand francs), ten years from now this city will have two hundred thousand inhabitants. There is already talk of building a street that will start at the obelisk at the end of the rue de Rome and run to the sea. By expanding toward the mountains in the direction of the rue Cannabière and the Allées de Meilhan, Marseilles has already reached Saint-Just. Apartments are dreadfully expensive and, as a result, Marseilles has omnibuses that go to all the villages in the environs (its future sub-

[35] Put the anecdote here if it is not already in the first two volumes.

*Caleche de Poste*

urbs) and all of them do extremely good business. It is true that horses and feed cost almost nothing.

A merchant who, to my knowledge, made one hundred thousand francs in Algiers, lives in Saint-Loup, a pretty village on the road to Toulon. Every morning, for ten sous the omnibus brings him to Marseilles and every afternoon, for ten sous, it takes him home again— when love of his club and gambling do not detain him until midnight. In that event he calls a barouche which takes him home for three francs. I saw him recently one evening at a very pleasant reception where there were a great many men and some very nice women, but none of them married. As he came out into a magnificent moonlight night, N. offered me a bed in the country. I accepted, but all night long, that is from three in the morning, the singing of birds kept me awake.

I have found an Italian theater here and again I endured the *Furioso* which, to my mind, does not have a single decent measure. I also saw *Norma* of which I like only the duet at the last, a duet sung à la Glück, whose poor commonplace *cantilena* is, no doubt, a steal. In the *Pirate* I found an accompaniment that portrays despair and a bit of melody that was equally good, but *remisso gradu*.

As far as lack of genius goes, Bellini has a slight advantage over Rossini. Rossini is too disguised, too agreeable even in the most tragic situations. Bellini is always crude, a peasant. Besides he was a very handsome man and he had a way with women.

Young Madame Marini reminds me of those nymphs painted on the walls in Pompeii. She has astonishing eyes and an even more astonishing wildness. Her acting is more or less haphazard, relying on the inspiration of the moment. Day before yesterday in the duet from *Norma*, she did all the foolish things a singer could and in the end she was so out of breath she could manage to sing only the principal notes but without joining them together.

There is a little tenor in this Italian company who sings as easily as one speaks and takes C sharp with chest notes. He is short and rather puny: I thought he pronounced the French of a Tyrolean girl very well. The men in the orchestra told me that Don Laborde is the son of a hairdresser from either Montpellier or Nîmes. He sings the lead and always in Italian. A very sickly, very thin man. Women will ruin this pretty voice.

*Victorine* or *The Dream*, a poor play, moved me to tears. The various events are announced but not portrayed on stage. Each intermission covers ten years in the life of the heroine, a kept girl, and the jokes are lacking in delicacy.

In spite of the rain I went to Saint-Just. Charming country houses; they now have trees around them. Each house is not more than two hundred paces from the next; one can always call the neighbor. But the road is like a prison; you travel between two walls eight to nine feet high. I enjoyed the view because I took the omnibus. In a barouche I would have seen only the walls.

Church of the Chartreux, beautiful because of its height. Architecture same as Saint Roch's.

The stock exchange has the advantage over most palaces in France of having a cornice. This façade is really not bad (in Rome or in Venice everyone would make fun of it).

I have just gone up to the first floor to see the paintings by Serre of the plague in 1720.[36] Contrary to my expectations I found them extremely good. I have been furious about the bad things Monsieur Millin had to say about these pictures, but that man was a sworn antiquarian and a member of forty-four academies as is plain to be seen on the title page of his books. A person like that knows everything that is prudent, useful and dull, but he does not know what is beautiful. Serre, whom he disparages from the height of his alleged knowledge, worked quickly because he was extremely poor. He did not belong to any academy and he was satisfied to do his duty, with all the fearlessness of a heart easily roused, at the time of the plague which he depicted in two paintings.

The larger picture is a cavalier treatment of a view (at an angle of 45 degrees) of the Cours. Far in the distance on the road from Aix where the arch of triumph now stands, one sees arches over which flowed water from the fountains of Marseilles. The concierge at the town hall told me he had seen some of the arches in his day. Now the water is siphoned under the road.

The courtyard, crowded with the sick and the dying, is a lifelike representation. In the foreground is the immortal Belzunce, bishop of Marseilles, who conducted himself as nobly as twenty other men, but in him any weakness would have been more harshly condemned. Such is fame in lands that do not have freedom of the press. On the right a corpse is being lowered by a rope from the fourth floor of a house. The men on horseback are city officials—Chevalier Roze, perhaps even Serre himself.

The second picture is smaller and shows the façade of the stock exchange. In Serre's painting the middle window, below the bust of Louis XIV, is higher than the others. I turned around to look at it and I verified that it is really lower.

---

[36] Paintings hung in a beautiful room, but the concierge has shrewdly covered them with a green cloth. The mayor should not tolerate this.

Serre has painted himself seated in a boat opposite the town hall, paintbrush in hand. He is wearing a wig and has a big nose like those in portraits belonging to the century of Louis XIV. What has become of those handsome noses? Look at the noses of our present-day aristocrats in portraits on the street corners! It would seem that the great king commanded the artists of his day to paint big noses.

As is natural this smaller painting is superior to the picture of the courtyard. Those extremely large spaces do not lend themselves to paintings. I noticed that in 1720, in Serre's day, the stock exchange did not have the four bas-reliefs above the ground floor.

The room in which I am writing these notes has not escaped the Minister of the Interior's gifts. He has presented it with a painting of Hannibal crossing the Alps *on horseback* and pointing out the plains of Italy to his soldiers. This painting should be given to some country parish which would see in it the martyrdom of a saint; for example send it to the fine church of Montréal near Carcassonne.

I looked again at the ignoble figure of Libertat. Unconsciously (or consciously) the sculptor has actually made a . . . , at the bottom of his heart, shamefully listing the honors which the great king, Henri IV, that keen judge and appreciator of talent, heaped upon him.

Serre's paintings, so modern and so true, make a pleasing contrast to that conceited Hannibal addressing his soldiers. They reminded me of the painting the committee refused to hang in the Louvre during the exposition of 1837. It was by Bard and I saw it at the Cercles des Arts. That painting of Bard's would not suffer by being placed near Serre's paintings.

# ·◦[ Marseilles, *May 15, 1838* ]◦·

This evening at the Gymnase, I saw a vaudeville act which the future historian of our present day will take particular note if, by chance, he is more than a mere phrasemaker and if he has learned to observe and interpret what he sees. This performance was the second act of *The Gamin from Paris*. I saw it captivate an audience of angry Marseillais, men and women who had just hissed off the stage an incredibly ugly old actor who was trying to play the part of the gamin. The furious storm of booing went on for twenty minutes. Twice the commissioner intervened. Finally, putting on his official sash he addressed the audience and at last obtained a moment of silence. The first act came to an end; the second act began promptly. Two minutes later that room, filled with men and women of Provence, was all attention and so silent you could have heard a wasp flying. The Russians would have had to kill half their people to quell a fanatical demonstration for equality. Never have I seen an audience tremble with deep emotion before a play as I did before this one. In the end everyone was weeping. The play is about the triumph of equality through the marriage of a poor girl, who has been seduced, to the son of a general, a peer of France.

## ·∘{ Marseilles, *May 16* }∘·

I am writing from Gémenos and the woods of Saint-Pons. Marseilles
has some really charming suburbs. The delightful green banks of the
Huveaune surpass, in my estimation, the green in the woods of Verrières for the simple reason that, on the banks of the Huveaune, shade is
a necessity; whereas in the woods of Verrières, it is only the image of
something which, in other places, is a delight. In the Verrières woods, I
spend three-quarters of the time searching for the sun.

How can I describe the sun in Marseilles to anyone who has not
seen it? I asked my traveling companion for an expression to describe
the woods of Saint-Pons. "Sweet memories of this Saint-Pons woods,"
he exclaimed, "with its deep shadows, the gurgle of water at the bottom
of the ravines, the soughing of wind through the branches, the charming play of light and shade at the foot of the high mountain, that vast
reservoir of the source. The water of this fountain springs from beds
carpeted with moss, basins where it bubbles over with fringes of foam,
ravines where it gleams through curtains of shade. Seated near the
source we catch a glimpse through the trees of the walls of some old
abbey green with lichens and mosses." My companion then pulled a
manuscript from his packet and read aloud the chronicle of Blanche de
Simiane . . .

One of the very pleasant members of that dreadful Department of
Health which I should like to see have its claws clipped, took me to
their office and to the guardroom. The sun is such a wonderful thing,
but so terrible in Marseilles that we have taken to avoiding the ugly
streets on the wrong side of the famous quai de la Bourse.[37]

The handsome large casement windows of the Department of
Health look out on the blue and shining sea three feet below them at
the entrance to the harbor. The office of these inquisitors is really the
most charming drawing room in Marseilles.

[37] Everyone—no, I am wrong—but people who are not too proud—a writer, for
instance, could live on this quay which is so conveniently situated, so full of life
and bursting with Southern gaiety, were it not for the horrible odor from the
harbor. The people of Marseilles should really sell the shirts off their backs to
clean up their harbor.

Facing the door as one enters is Puget's *Plague of Milan*. Details true, interesting and varied. This bas-relief by that great artist is really a picture just as our modern pictures are really bas-reliefs. This one has surprising depth. It is a long distance from the leg of that plague-stricken man in the foreground to the woman flinging herself over the body of her husband who has just died of the plague. And how gravely that good saint Charles Borromeo gazes up to heaven. The Saint Charles in the bas-relief is not like the real Saint Charles either in physique or in morale. He had that big nose, natural to his long face. He was young and determined. Whatever he may have thought about the goodness of God who sent the plague, or rather allowed it to come to these people, the good saint never stopped looking up to heaven. He went to the aid of the sick and administered the sacraments to the dying with the same ardor with which he used formerly to intrigue in the conclave.

Puget was worthy to portray such a subject. Like Serre he, too, would have risked his life. His bas-relief (as little low relief as possible) does not have the decided outline of the antique. Those overly sharp outlines are absurd for anything in the background. But bas-relief is a poor genre, good only when used for inscriptions.

This masterpiece of Puget's was bought by the Health and Sanitation Department only after the artist's death, May 25, 1730, at the moment when Puget's grandson was about to send it abroad to be sold. What chance brought about in 1730 should serve as a general rule: never to buy the works of living artists.

The paintings that surrounded Puget's bas-relief have been collected on the opposite principle. And heaven knows how they will be judged a century from now. . . .

To the left of the bas-relief is a famous painting of the Madonna, Saint Roch and some victims of the plague. It was painted by David in Rome around 1780. Compared to the works of Restout, Van Loo and Coypel, it is a masterpiece. The naked figure in the background is not bad; the drawing is good and does not lack strength but all the flesh tones are gray. This is a forerunner of Ingres's coloring. The Madonna has a slightly reddish tinge.

To the right of the Puget, Gérard has painted Monsignor de Belzunce distributing bread to the unfortunate victims. That great and witty man presented Marseilles with this painting. On the subject of gifts, I was told about the compulsory gift he was obliged to make, but we shall speak of that later on.

Opposite the casement windows stands the bust of the young French physician, Mazet, whose zeal led him to Barcelona during the yellow fever. The king made a present of this painting to the Health and Sanitation Administration, but out of consideration, I shall refrain from naming the artist.

Paul Guérin painted the self-sacrifice of Chevalier Roze on his way to remove one thousand two hundred corpses that had lain on La Tourette esplanade for two weeks. Outraged by this horrible danger, that great-hearted man discovered that two ancient wells with outlets on the sea were empty. There he had the sad remains carried. Roze was only a plain citizen. It was Monsignor de Belzunce who was acclaimed as the hero of the plague and whose praises the Abbé Delille sang.

Two hundred soldiers, three hundred prisoners whom Roze led, recoiled in horror.

"What's this, my lads!" cried Roze and, dismounting, he picked up a corpse in his arms. All the prisoners, with the exception of two, were dead in three days. Roze came out of it with only a slight illness.

Arrived in Toulon on the 17th at five o'clock in a driving rain.

Up at three o'clock. I was tired, in despair. I lay down on the sofa in a small but very clean room, English style, and I slept until eight o'clock. There was nothing to be had at the hotel at this unseemly hour so, trying to avoid the rain and a stream of clear water three feet wide, I went to a shady-looking café where I was treated with the utmost politeness. In contrast to the utter but coarse naturalness of this provincial land, the courtesy of the mother and young daughter who ran this café next to the Pomme et Cloche d'Or, delighted me.

At the door where I was forced to wait because of the driving rain, I found an American, a very moral mulatto, who was instructing a little bootblack. The American's servant, a lad of fifteen and equally moral, amused me and at the same time aroused my pity. In the end the eight-year-old bootblack, bored with the Americans, simply walked off and left them.

On arising, a brief glimpse of the sun but soon a fine rain and strong west wind. What was to become of me? I had no umbrella and only two shirts. When I left Marseilles I had intended to go only as far as La Ciotat. With my thoughts constantly on forming an opinion of the

---

[38] Written in Toulon at the Croix d'Or. I had no time to copy in ink all my penciled notes on my delightful trip to Grasse. Here, at least, is the itinerary:

May 16th at two o'clock, I set out for La Ciotat. Strange road after Aubagne. Arrived in La Ciotat at night: no coffee fit to drink.

May 17th. At quarter-past three went to the beach to breathe in the lukewarm air of the morning; finest sensation of the whole journey since Paris.

At four o'clock, departure for Aubagne. Arrived at eight o'clock. I strolled about, doubtful of finding a seat. Monsieur Barthelon, typical scholar's face. Most horrible smell of smoke my nose has ever encountered. At ten o'clock departure for Toulon; in the coach with me, a country fellow with a narrow head and a native of Marseilles. I slept all the way through the *Gorges d'Ollioules* through which the old main road passes. Raining in torrents; superb countryside; handsome plane trees at Ollioules and in this village on the way down to Toulon. It was raining so hard that I left the Croix d'Or toward half-past nine only to go to a very elegant café to get a cup of coffee with milk.

May 18th. In spite of the rain I keep going. Intestinal trouble. I make my day memorable by daring to go to La Seyne in a vile mistral that was just beginning, but it turns out that there was no sea running and only the sea affects steamboats. Cost: four sous there and the same to return. Skipper on the way over very polite. The . . . tried to draw me into conversation. I prefer to meditate.

*Toulon: Seen from Fort Lamalgue*

country and describing it, I become completely absent-minded—with the most baneful results.

I then visited the battlefield and the harbor. The great trees on the battlefield are very handsome, most of them plane trees, but I was shocked to see a green shutter in the Port Admiral's garden. How hideous! There should have been iron bars.

At the harbor, pursued by rain and a violent west wind, I took refuge in a smart-looking café. Coffee very poor! The waiter admitted as much to four young men, and yet the café was very elegant with wainscotting and moldings. I was uncertain whether to take the little steamboat to La Seyne, but I told myself that the weather could not possibly be worse this afternoon.

Toulon, a city given over to the practical and the useful, with straight and narrow streets, would be very ugly without its plane trees. It is true the trees have been strangely mutilated, but without them there would be no shade.

Very pretty boulevard called rue Lafayette: pavements twelve feet wide, very well paved with field bricks. The carriage road in the center is convex and paved with fine square stones larger than the Fontainebleau paving stones used in Paris. The pavements are lined with handsome plane trees growing out of the bricks with, beyond the trees, a border of large stones beside a swift-flowing stream of clear water as in Tarbes.

The general effect must be delightful in summer in this land of dust and dazzling light. Day before yesterday, on the way from Marseilles to Aubagne, the light and the whiteness of the roads really hurt my eyes. Toulon has several little squares crowded with plane trees that hide the sky. There are any number of pretty, though not elaborate, fountains in this city. At the end of the narrow street that leads to the harbor, beside Puget's famous caryatids, a fountain made from a small obelisk surmounted by two very beautiful heads conjoined like the heads of Janus, gives a remarkable effect of a handsome antique.

For a long time I stood there gazing respectfully at the two statues by Puget. It was hard to read the date on the balcony, 1657 I think it was. Fortunately there are two hundred leagues between Paris and Toulon. These caryatids are far removed from the stupidities Le Brun was soon to scatter around Paris. Festoons of flowers from the center of the balcony join together those two grotesquely masked figures. That wealth of flowers seems to me in poor taste. It is this mania for garlands of flowers which is the distinguishing mark of the poor and slipshod architecture of the Louis XV period. Moreover Puget's charming naturalism was not what was needed here. There should have been the strength of Michelangelo, something like that admirable slave on the ground floor of the Louvre, under the clock.

But this naturalism is like Rossini's delicious *cantilena* sung to the judge's atrocious words in the *Gazza ladra*. Speaking of a stolen envelope which is going to doom the young girl to be hanged, the judge (to whom she has refused to yield and who, in his rage, takes his revenge) cries: *"Vuol dir lo stesso!"*

Pardon this long comparison. I meant that beauty created by men like Rossini and Puget is a hundred times better than the merely appropriate work produced by those artists who should be called craftsmen and whose real talent lies in pleasing the department head who authorizes their work.

I confess I am not a good traveler and the reader does not need my admission of this obvious fact. In this gloomy weather, this tiresome rain and disagreeable wind, I could not bring myself to visit the great naval establishment, the Caducée, etc. . . .

Above all I have a horror of meeting convicts. Ugliness in any form depresses me. I, who endure the fatigues of the stagecoach and uncomfortable bedrooms, in the hope of stumbling upon something beautiful! But I should not complain. I shall never forget the sight of the sea at three o'clock in the morning, day before yesterday in La Ciotat. That sight is equal to the most beautiful views from the Monti di Brianza and the lakes north of Milan which sent me into such absurd transports of joy in the years from 1814 to 1821 when I was madly in love with painting—and a number of other things (Angelina, Mathilde D.).

Deeply moved though I am by the memory of that dawn in La Ciotat, today I feel the keenest sorrow at the sight of anything ugly. There are consequently many things I cannot look at. Sometimes merely to feel scorn is a torture to me, and anyone who knows the France of 1838 will do me the justice to admit that it takes a lot of skill to avoid being bored to death by scorn.

What stories about well paid magistrates have I not heard on my journey from Bordeaux to Bayonne, Pau, Narbonne, Montpellier and Marseilles! When I am older and more hardened, these sad stories will appear in my *History of My Time*. But what shabby conduct, what ugliness! Has the world always been so corrupt, so base, so brazenly hypocritical? Am I worse than other men? Am I envious? Where, for instance, do I get this inordinate desire to have that magistrate from . . . given a sound thrashing? And that man makes such a pre-possessing appearance in Paris drawing rooms! He can even tell a story with a certain charm. But what has he not done to this little town of three thousand inhabitants! When people read this sketch, I am sure they will think he humiliated me, hurt my pride, in Paris! If I allowed myself to print such things, the world would think this "diary" was written by Juvenal.

Fortunately for me, after I have written them, I forget them completely. They come back to mind only when I see the names of those men on the front page of the newspaper. What scoundrels they are!

One of them—the gentlest, the most charming of men who, if you were to see him in a Paris drawing room, looks like an abbé of the Ancien Régime—ordered innocent people whom not even the breath of suspicion could touch, sent to the guillotine. I look at him often in astonishment. He made that decision lightly, as lightly as if he were choosing the color of a piece of furniture. It is the memory of that worldly cleric that makes my heart sink at the sight of certain infamous deeds dated 1838. There was no political bloodshed under Louis Philippe; but if the morals of 1816 were to return, those men whose names I refrain from mentioning would make blood flow just as easily as they now play knavish tricks while, at the same time, talking virtue and morality.

The vast and gloomy pitfall I must constantly avoid, for it would ruin forever the slight interest this journey of mine might arouse in minds haunted by fear, is SCORN.

If I can publish my *History of My Time* the reader will judge for himself what low, contemptible, beastly and hypocritical things I have had the misfortune to hear on this journey and frequently to verify. I have wasted entire days in very ugly places and the anecdotes I heard have sometimes made me shrink from verifying a single fact. But even as a judge I could not condemn; I have not reached that certainty.

*Toulon: Seaside*

Today, dogged by that foul rain, I went twice to the reading room. I was very bored. At last, toward three o'clock, I remembered what General Michaud told me he had seen the night before; a soldier, who was fleeing and despised himself for it, pulled his horse up short, changed the cartridge caps in his pistols, rode his horse off the road behind a hedge, killed one enemy, wounded another and by so doing halted a disorderly rout which could soon have had disastrous results.

"Tomorrow," the General told him, "you will be a corporal and, before the end of the year, a sergeant-major."

That man deserved to have been made second-lieutenant before the end of the campaign.

How, after so magnificent a. . . . shall I dare to admit that I managed to rid my day of boredom by boarding the steamboat at three o'clock just when the rainstorm had driven the passengers below decks? The wind, blowing in violent gusts, flung the rain in my face. I had to hold on to my hat. This bay of Toulon, the size of a small lake, was as rough as could be. And yet, though the boat did not pitch and toss, it took us one hour to reach the pretty little town of La Seyne.

I was much entertained by the gallantry of a sailor toward a very pretty woman from a well-to-do lower-class family. The heat had driven her and another woman from the cabin below deck. He arranged a sail as a shelter for her and her baby, but the violent wind tore it away. As he put the sail back again, he tickled the pretty traveler and, while pretending to cover her, he uncovered her. There was so much gaiety, so much naturalness and even charm in this little byplay which went on for an hour only a foot and a half away from me. The other woman, who was not being courted, turned her attention to me. "This gentleman is getting wet," she said. I should have talked with her for she was a handsome creature, but the sight of the flirtation gave me more pleasure. The pretty woman warded off the sailor as best she could. To one of his first compliments, a word with a double meaning, she answered sharply: "*Merde!*"

La Seyne, a pretty little town of eight thousand souls, so the owner of the café told me—he may have been lying—a nice place for an impoverished man to settle down. It has none of the beauty of several places I know; for example, Sestri di Levante between Genoa and Sarzana. But here we are in France, no chance of being annoyed by the

priest or by the local police. I am supposing, of course, that the poor
devil reduced to an income of eighteen hundred francs who would retire to La Seyne, would go to Mass and would take the sacrament at
Easter.

Good conversation with a ship's corporal (forty-two francs a
month) who was on his way home from Algiers and should be given
the Cross. He has just left after twenty-four years of service. In spite of
the rain I saw a number of fine steamboats under construction.

Our return to Toulon, favored by a wild west wind, was swift. The
sailors had hoisted a sail. The outing cost four sous.

I tried to study or rather to apply to the terrain the story of the
siege of Toulon that I have written. But the tremendous number of
forts around this roadstead is staggering. Moreover they change their
names every ten years depending upon the government then in power
in Paris. When I studied in Toulon in 1828, several of these forts had
other names.

The water in the harbor is clear and it does not smell bad. The quay
is broader than the charming Quai de la Bourse in Marseilles, but it
faces in almost the same direction. A merchant I know told me that in
winter it is freezing cold on this quay because of the north wind. In
Marseilles the Quai de la Bourse is a little Provence, as they say in the
North and, in winter, the water in the harbor has almost no odor.

I was delighted when the mistral began to blow. I saw it making up
as I was on my way back from La Seyne. As we came out of that
town's pretty little harbor, the sky was so dark that by the time we
entered the harbor of Toulon, we could barely distinguish the place in
the sky where the sun had been. At that moment the mistral set all the
doors to banging and on the street people were already bundled in
coats.

At the table d'hôte I dined opposite some good-looking officers
from Paris who leave tomorrow for Africa. The almost unconscious
fatuousness of these gentlemen in their conversation with a very decent
naval officer! This natural and very simple sailor is just back from Africa where he has been a number of times. He is sunburned and has all
the easy good nature of a German. He made a mistake in the name of a
general in command of a station in Africa. Tremendous scorn with
which the gentlemen from Paris challenged him sharply, in a politely

*Toulon: Bureaux de la Marine*

*Toulon: Entrance to the Port*

commiserating tone as if to say: "Good Lord! How can anyone make such a mistake?" The poor sailor caught the tone but did not know how to defend himself.

"But gentlemen, I've seen the generals we come in contact with in Oran, Bône and Bougie change at least forty times. So we decided not to pay any attention to their names. We just say: the general from Bône. If one of them had won a battle we wouldn't forget his name. But after six months in those posts they fall ill and disappear, etc. etc."

He should have said something of that sort. But, chilled by the deep commiseration his blunder had called forth, the naval officer refused to give the Parisians any more information. Those young officers, courageous and eager for battle though they were, were terribly afraid of fever. A certain ill-chosen camp had been the cemetery for two-thirds of the regiment encamped there—I shall not give the number of that regiment. There was a perfectly healthy site and, from a military point of view, one equally as good, only ten minutes from the fatal camp where the general's stupidity had cost the lives of eight hundred men. It never occurred to these gleaming young officers that when you camp under the lee of the desert wind and to the north of a swamp over which the wind blows you are sure to be poisoned even if you were on a mountain. Fever often does not appear until twenty days later. You can catch it even a hundred leagues from the site. Bleeding is fatal. We, who have lived in hot climates, know that. The little naval officer who looked like a subaltern was about to tell them all that when he was silenced by their air of profound pity because he had forgotten the name of an unknown general. This comedy amused me.

A young civilian from Paris tried to impress us by his elegant manner. He had a remarkably aquiline nose and a forehead at once bulging and yet receding, a typical face of the Louis XIV era to which haughtiness seems natural (like Commodore Guibert in the stagecoach from Tarbes to Auch where the passengers talked so much nonsense).

All the streets in Toulon that are not parallel to the harbor are on an incline and all of them have two swiftly flowing streams. From all sides, in moments of silence, one hears the gurgling of running water. I have not seen a single carriage. Only in front of my hotel (in the provinces you never say inn) and beneath the tall plane trees which completely hide the first floors of the houses opposite, there are eight or ten stage-coaches.

Behind the earthen arsenal on the ramparts there are some plane trees on which, at a height of fifteen feet, one might establish salons of twenty persons as they do in the cafés in Brunswick, Leipzig, etc. At first cut horizontally to give shade, the vertical branches have been allowed to grow when it was no longer necessary to think about shade.

Every large building built by the government has some enormously stupid mistake in it. As I did on my way to La Seyne, I visited the great hospital of Saint Mandrier's opposite Toulon on the other side of the roadstead and I asked a sailor what they were going to do with it.

"Well, sir, there's not a soul there; it is wide open to the mistral. It's uninhabitable."

"And yet," I pointed out, "in case of the plague or the yellow fever, Saint Mandrier's would be disinfected by the mistral . . ."

Left Toulon at half-past nine. They had told me between eight forty-five and nine o'clock. I smoked my cigar beneath those plane trees whose shadow covers the fifteen or twenty stagecoaches drawn up opposite the Croix d'Or.

Superb weather which we owe to the mistral. Provence is delightful in the month of May. This Champs de Mars in Toulon, which I have never seen except when covered by half a foot of dust and with its trees powdered white, is charming today. A little stream flows at the foot of the plane trees and waters them just as on the new boulevards in Marseilles.

Toulon is about to acquire a large suburb in the direction of La Vallette.

Liveliness of my two traveling companions who, forsaking all dignity, told me about their love affairs. They are health officers, often employed on ships. One of them has been to see his mistress in Toulon and is dying from the cold today.

# ·⊰[ Cuers, *May 19, 1838* ]⊱·

We changed horses at Cuers, that is to say we spent a long half hour there. Now that this coach has won out over its competitors, it often travels at a snail's pace.

At Cuers, I ate cherries for the first time this year. This little town would be rather ugly if it were not for the plane trees. The gorgeous plane tree planted in front of the town hall is definitely an ornament. Magnificent sound of the bell. I went into the church; nothing could be duller; Gothic feathered arch; nave shaped like a tennis court. The square is not bad because of the great trees.

On the coach we were joined by a very shrewd peasant who appeared to be ill. He looked like Jules. Farther along a third doctor got in. He told us about his chaste relations with the nineteen-year-old Greek wife of an officer who was stationed in Algiers. (The doctor was blind in one eye.)

For the first time I am seeing a bit of the countryside in Provence that is not covered with dust. The soil consists of three feet of earth on a reddish rock which shows through the dirt. We traveled with the mountain on our left. Here and there the road was torn up to allow the little streams from the mountain to flow through. Those upturned pieces made rough going, jolting the stagecoach as we bumped along.

I was delighted to see a perfectly green mountain covered with grass to the summit, a rare sight in Provence. The beauty of the olive trees in Puget surprised me; I say beauty though there are no uglier trees in the world. They always look dispeptic and crippled, but here in Puget, they are large. My traveling companions explained that of all the olive trees in Provence, these are the only ones that do not freeze.

# ·◦[ Grasse, *Sunday, May 20* ]◦·

Yesterday, while half asleep at Draguignan, this thought struck me: I had only forty-six francs left when I opened my roll to pay the woman at the stagecoach (the widow Boivin whose husband has recently departed this life at the age of thirty-eight by dint of having lived up to his name [wine drinker] too well. To tell the truth he drank brandy instead of wine. She is an orderly, methodical woman. She sent for me and mockingly refused a tip of fifteen sous).

| | |
|---|---|
| Therefore, balance of | 46 francs |
| Sunday dinner | 2.50 |
| Tips | 1. |
| Room | 2. |
| Laundry | ·0.75 |
| Sunday lunch | 1. |
| Journey | 6. |
| | 13.25 |
| Balance remaining | 33 francs |

Is that enough for me to go to Fréjus? I would not be able to stop at Toulon and would have to hurry on in spite of weariness.

Disgust. My first time in Grasse (pretty servant girl).

For a very long time, twenty or twenty-five years, I have always suffered a moment of profound disgust an hour after arriving in a new town and the more charming the picture I had formed, the more my imagination had dwelt upon it, the keener and more painful that moment of disgust is sure to be.

Here in Grasse, May 20th, 1838, I have only now realized why. When I arrive in a town I have never visited before, I am obliged to cope with petty, mundane details: to look for a café, for a room, to make sure I am not cheated. All these horrid nuisances distract me from my delightful meditations.

There are, therefore, any number of hindrances one would like to have removed and now, for the first time in eight years, I was forced to think of economizing. I had only forty-six francs left with which to get

239

back to Marseilles. Why hadn't I brought two hundred francs with me? Why didn't I always carry ten napoleons sewed into my belt? The trouble is that when my imagination catches fire I yield to the pleasure of meditating and forget all about the necessary daily tasks.

Arrived in Draguignan at eleven o'clock and left at two in the morning after having been in bed exactly one hour and a half. The coach struck me as a rather ramshackle affair it was so hard and the road so rough. Over streets torn up and filled with stones from the recent rains, we traveled at a fast trot. Those hateful blocks of broken road gave me such a headache that I left the compartment and took refuge in the boot which by good luck was empty. Wretched mountain scenery; fields covered with stones. I was dead for sleep and completely exhausted.

Toward half-past nine, after crossing one river and climbing an endless mountain we came again to cultivated land; low, sustaining walls piled one above the other. I counted as many as twelve of them forming a sort of system; to tell the truth they were only two or three feet high. The fields were full of olive trees, fig trees and mulberry trees. The patience those poor peasants have to use in arranging the stones! In Geneva this is called Canaan farming, for they must always bring the Bible into everything. Many people in that country have seen the land of Canaan from the riviera of Genoa (Lullin's letters on Italy, very sound except for Canaan).

As we approached Grasse, the color of the leaves on the olive trees took on a deeper green; the trees themselves were as large as willows. The fig trees are often eight inches around the trunk, exactly like the trees on the road to Portici. That is because Grasse is sheltered from the north by a mountain that is bare on top. At last I have seen rose bushes cultivated in the open. The wind was from the south and rolling up enormous clouds; I fear we shall have rain.

Suddenly I saw Grasse, flat against a little hill and surrounded by other hills covered with olive trees that looked as though they were about to hurl themselves down on the town. This town is completely Genoese in character. Never have I seen anything in miniature more reminiscent of Genoa and its coastal towns.

We were high above the sea which seemed to be two miles away. On arriving in Grasse, we found a terrace filled with great trees, far

*Grasse*

more beautiful than the trees of Saint-Germain. On the right and on the left, mountains literally covered to their summits with tufted olive trees and, down below, a vast expanse of sea which, as the bird flies, does not seem to be more than two miles away.

I was told that this town is filled with clubs which makes it very unpleasant for a stranger. No regular café. I had the greatest trouble in finding a way to read the latest number of the *Débats*.

Narrow streets as in the towns on the shore around Genoa. The farming would make one think we were in Sestri or Nervi, but with a total absence of architecture and cafés and the bad odor in the streets where they are always making a little manure heap after the execrable custom I had already met in Aubagne and in Luc.[39]

They do not need an aqueduct here. At the highest part in town a fine stream of water rises out of the ground. I spent a long time gazing at this sight from the top of the parapet that overlooks the source. There is no luxury here, I was told. A man with a fortune of a hundred thousand francs wears a threadbare coat; and Grasse numbers several millionaires, all as poorly dressed as the rest of its citizens. On the other hand, the lower middle class who, today (Sunday), throng the magnificent terrace, all look very well-to-do.

The prettiest site on this terrace, the one where, if we were in Italy, there would be any number of cafés, is occupied by the general hospital. I admit the need for a hospital, but it should be built outside of the town and the present building restored to civilization. If the inhabitants were wealthy, this would be the place for them to meet and enjoy themselves.

Here again is a town where a poor man might choose to take refuge: Granville or Grasse; down there, civilization, exchange of ideas; here, the climate and the charming tillage of the soil; moreover, the poor devil would not be bothered by the wealth of other men as in Granville. I say that to ease my conscience for, in my eyes, a man should settle a hundred feet from the sea and not two leagues away. And then the smallest town on the coast of Genoa is a hundred times superior to this one, but here we are in France and we do not have to

[39] Beneath my window in Grasse, remains of that elegant Gothic that preceded the Renaissance. Is there a black Gothic, sad and severe, in Provence, so near Arles, Fréjus, and Nîmes?

think about the government. The newspaper arrives from Paris five days late.

In reality even in my room I am haunted by a certain smell of resin which gives me a headache. It could well be the scent from the Grasse perfumery.[40]

[40] Above Grasse near route 3337 which must lead to Digne, a waterfall.

Desirable location. Here, I said to myself, a man who detests the nuisance of passports could spend the evening of his life in peace. From the top of my tilbury I looked enviously at the charming white villas surrounded by tall olive trees and oak groves that crown the mountain to the east of Cannes. But I had counted "without the falcon of cruel talons."

That hidden venom, which seems to make a point of poisoning the most charming places on the Mediterranean, also attacks this charming mountain. A Monsieur Dumas (he is from Dieppe) has been obliged to have the ancient elms that shade his chateau cut down. He had been told this would let in more air and would prevent fever. Unhealthy stagnant waters, far from there and much lower down behind the point of land that juts out toward the island of Sainte-Marguerite on the Golfe Juan which has become so famous, have poisoned this whole mountain. In times past, half of Cannes suffered from fever in the month of August. At last it occurred to the authorities to clean up a little river that flows to the east of Cannes, and the fever disappeared. All the same, household waters and the three cesspools of Cannes poison the pretty promenade along the sea.

Lord Brougham had his charming little villa built on the west of the promontory crowned by the church of Cannes, Notre-Dame-d'Espérance, beyond the river Riou which is spanned by a bridge over which I

[41] Arrived at two o'clock Monday, May 21st. It rained a little every hour, but sunny in between. Stopping at the Hôtel du Midi (Monsieur Gimbert, obliging landlord, but no view; house faces south). I came from Grasse in a tilbury; in my opinion it is the only way to travel. I found . . . who took me to the Roman bridge and the valley of the Riou which they are enlarging very scientifically for a pier which is to be 250 to 260 métres long (nine hundred thousand francs voted). The Seguin brothers are the contractors—three hundred workmen; almost none from this part of the country; they are Piedmontese and they earn twenty-five to forty-five sous a day.
One of the Seguin brothers lost his wife of twenty-three years here. They say he is an authority in Vienne now.
Good dinner at Monsieur Gimbert's. Excellent water. Trip to the Riou. Roman bridge. After dinner, I climbed up to the church. On the door I read: "Consecrated in 1643." The arcades in chapels were still pointed in 1643.
Most beautiful stones from this region.
I joked with two rather pretty young girls of fourteen. Births announced by the town crier.

have just had the honor to cross. Its antiquity is the only thing in its favor. It is built of flat little stones and to tell the truth it is so horribly *bourgeois*, so lacking in everything that stirs the imagination, so different from the bridge at Vaison that I had difficulty in believing it was Roman.

Cannet, a village behind Cannes, ten minutes from Cannes and from the sea, where I saw orange trees growing in the open and also beginning to form hedges.[42]

---

[42] On May 22nd, at six o'clock I must leave for Le Luc where we arrive at six o'clock. At ten o'clock, we leave for Toulon where we arrive on the 23rd at seven o'clock in the morning, and that evening at six o'clock in Marseilles.

*Cannes*

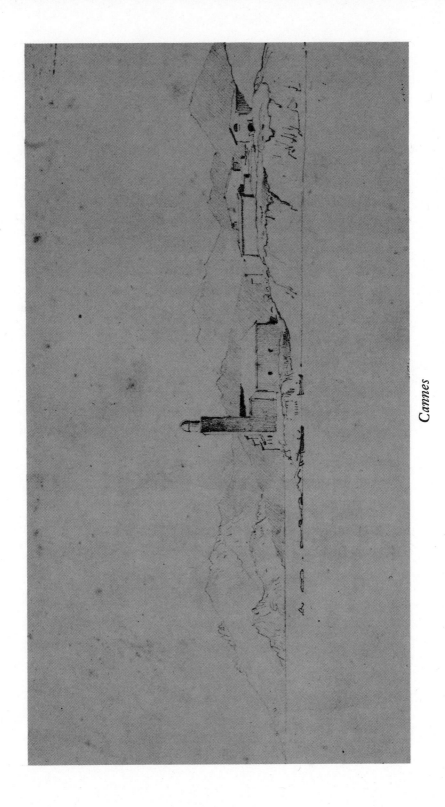

*Cannes*

Ascension Day. Day and sun magnificent. This evening, a tremendous crowd at the Gymnase to see Mademoiselle Séral dance. Spanish dances. Spanish women are so well liked in France because they show so much *brio*, which vanity makes impossible in France and *brio*, which would be so ridiculous in Paris, is the epitome of joy.

There was a dance of jealousy between peasants which aroused great excitement; someone threw a wreath of flowers on the stage. What ignoble gestures!

How surprised Mademoiselle Chameroy would be to see things like that applauded! The reader, born perhaps in 1812, does not know that, around the year 1804 Mademoiselle Chameroy was a charming dancer who died at the beginning of the Consulate. To test the government of the First Consul the priests refused to bury her.

When we are very old and are obliged to leave this world, we can never imagine what people will be doing thirty years after us. There is nothing simpler: they will be doing exactly the contrary of what they were doing in our day. I imagined the charming Chameroy watching Mademoiselle Séral and hearing her applauded. And let there be no mistake: Mademoiselle Chameroy would be just as shocked by the charms of the lovely Elssler[43] in the *Lame Devil* as by Mademoiselle Séral and perhaps much more so. For she would have wit enough to perceive that Mademoiselle Elssler was as superior to her as the poems of Lamartine are to those of the Abbé Delille which society was so mad about in 1804.

[43] Fanny Elssler (1810–1884): youngest daughter of Johann Elssler, copyist and servant of Haydn. She danced at the Paris Opera (1834–39) and also in London and became a great favorite in both cities. In 1841 she made a triumphal tour of the United States. (Translator's note)

# ⋅⋅◦[ Marseilles, *May 27* ]◦⋅⋅

Grand parade under the shade of the beautiful trees on the allées de Meilhan. The colonels are getting too fat to wage war. How could they run through the Rivoli vineyards on the Genoa riviera with those big paunches? Can a man who has passed forty-five fight a war? Every man in the army of Italy that crossed the bridge at Lodi was no more than twenty-five years old. The commander-in-chief, who was twenty-seven, was older than nine-tenths of his soldiers. Genius and youth: *sic itur ad astra.*

# ·=][ Vaison ][=·

As we crossed the bridge over the river Ouvèze, I noticed the broad and charming valley this river opens in the mountains and caught a glimpse of the hill behind which lies Vaison that I visited with such pleasure . . . years ago.

The low rooms of the Avignon museum are filled with ancient odds and ends found in Vaison. The principal exhibits are eight to ten feet high, a species of niches belonging to fountains and monuments like the monument of the Abbé Barthélmy in Aubagne. On these monuments are bas-reliefs that are abominably designed. Beside them kneels King René, and behind him his chancellor or his counselor. The whole thing is life-size and so ugly that I attribute its fame to some German artist.

# ·⊰[ Valence ]⊱·

Arrived June 1st, 1838, at one o'clock in the morning. Valence is a sordid town and, above all, paved with nasty little pointed stones not filled in with sand, which makes walking a serious problem to which you must give all your attention.

By good fortune an open space has been left between the suburbs and the town. They should plant it with eight rows of plane trees as they did in Marseilles, but in France big cities are a century or two ahead of the little ones. I am convinced that the chief magistrate of Valence thinks it is much more beautiful not to have a single tree from the end of the Saunière quarter (suburb of Avignon) to the Rhone and the wire bridge. The Frenchman of the old school—the Frenchman whose character this literature delineates—has no liking for natural beauties, whereas the Englishman's love of nature is his real delight, next only to his instinct to fight obstacles and never to forget his rank.

All the public buildings that have been built in Valence are therefore almost absurd. At this moment they are completing a rather decent though somewhat cumbersome law court but on the whole—in view of this town's position five hundred leagues from Italy—not at all bad. Unfortunately they have tucked it away in the gloomiest little street in Valence (and that is saying a great deal) where, without doubt, land was once very dear. It would have appeared so simple to a German magistrate to put this building in a field on the way to the bridge a hundred feet from the town wall which is open on all sides and alongside of some inns and popular cafés; in other words, close to the everyday life of the town. The building would have been seen from afar by almost all the steamboats coming down the Rhone and would have done honor to the town. And what is more important you could have breathed fresh air there! A quarter of an hour ago I heard a case pleaded in those law courts. The bad air drove me away. The judges who spend their lives in that mephitic atmosphere have never looked in a chemistry dictionary for the word "ventilator." And this is a new building not yet completed! Moreover to reach their seats the lawyers have to pass through the crowd and I had the honor to be stoutly elbowed by a gentleman with a conceited air, dressed in black, who was on his way to his bench. It would have been so simple to copy the law courts in England, but do these gentlemen even know there is an England?

The theater should have been put in the center of the town. In the winter on a chilly, rainy night, people go to bed at eleven o'clock. The theater is not bad. It is naturally small as befits the town, but it has a much finer façade than the façade of the theater in Marseilles, though not so good as the one in Avignon and not nearly so good as the one in Le Havre. There should have been a covered promenade on the right wing even had they been obliged to put up wooden columns for the sake of economy. They should also have had a delightful café like the one in Bordeaux.

Very pretty little church of Saint Apollinaire. Not one pointed arch, everything semicircular in shape. Very wide center nave separated from the side aisles by slender shafts of four semi-attached columns in a square pillar. The only thing Gothic about these columns is their extreme height. The attached column on the side toward the main nave rises to a greater height than the columns on the three other sides. All around, particularly at the crosspieces of the Latin Cross (which is also the shape of Saint Apollinaire's) there are a number of little semicircular windows with Corinthian columns, reminiscent of the amphitheaters in Roman architecture. This church was formerly dedicated to two saints who lost their rights when Saint Apollinaire, bishop of Valence was buried there around the year 500, I think. The present church dates from . . . (see the *Gallia christiana*).

Saint Apollinaire's has been painted an off-white bordering on light gray; it is not yet the natural color (the color time has given Saint Jacques de la Boucherie and which you can see from a distance), but it is infinitely superior to the disgusting buff color of Notre-Dame in Paris, Saint Sulpice, etc.

The entrance is through the side aisles; it looks to me as though a huge square tower, the same style as the church and standing on the spot where the portal should have been, has been torn down. I caught a glimpse in the choir of good copies of Andrea del Sarto and especially of Guido Reni. An *Ascension*, a modern painting, melodramatic in style, looks very well at the back of the choir which is separated by a solid wall from the nave. In this place there is a plethora of little Corin-

*Valence*

*Valence*

thian columns and semicircular arches as in charming Saint Sernin's in Toulouse.

Saint Apollinaire's seemed to me quite lovely and it was far from dark; nor was it gloomy and ugly like so many excellent little churches in the North of France. The style of the architect who built Saint Apollinaire's was somewhat spoiled by memories of the light in pagan edifices: he did not think of hell often enough.

A good bust of Pius VI; he looks commonplace. Very good likeness. Several windows have colored glass in them; I certainly did not miss the gloomy pictures in colored glass of which I saw some masterpieces at Auch (those works really made for fourteenth-century spectators offend the eye with their ridiculous sheen. They have no luminous center, etc. . . .). But it had not occurred to me that the absence of that setting, beside which . . . is a model of elegance, makes a church look like a barbershop. I noticed this in Saint Apollinaire's. An early June sun was pouring in through the colored panes painting the whole church with the hues of the rainbow. Near the north door was a little square structure with several semicircular arches, a fairly good cornice and four almost Corinthian columns at the four corners. Not until I stood there did I notice that the handsome tower opposite the spot where the church portal should be, was being torn down.

On the Place des Clercs, alongside of the church, I saw that in Valence cornices project properly, a thing so lacking in the houses in Bayonne and the very thing that makes them look so ridiculous.

Near this square stood a little house with its façade completely covered with swirls and ornaments in the flamboyant Gothic style, and in addition any number of busts and statues. This was far removed from the elegance of the house opposite the cathedral in Rouen or from certain parts of the House of Parliament. There is something noble, lacking in common sense and chivalrous in that architecture in Rouen; it reminds a man who has attained nothing higher than the emoluments and functions of a sub-prefect, of the heroes of Ariosto (but does a manufacturer from Rouen ever think of a madman like Ariosto?). The architecture in Valence is commonplace. The faces of the idlers I saw on the suspension bridge, slouching along to give themselves airs, speak more eloquently to the imagination than the serious, preoccupied air of Rouen merchants rushing off to business.

Very fine bridge, rather grand and impressive. It has a single support in the middle of the river and at that point a very pretty triumphal arch in hewn stone. I found the style a little too severe and close to the Renaissance style. These triumphal arches on suspension bridges will discredit the real arches of triumph. They are much better located in general, but a monument as useless as an arch of triumph owes part of its merit to its rarity. For example, the traveler who journeyed this morning from Lyons to Arles at six miles an hour has seen twenty arches of triumph—several of them, like the one in Valence, really quite good. But he would not go twenty steps to see the arch of triumph on the Carrousel (in Paris).

The Crussol rock, opposite the bridge, is horribly ugly; it is falling in ruins, a ruin that has nothing to offer but sheer ugliness. The shore opposite Valence is equally flat and ugly. Perhaps a hundred years from now some man of good taste who has come to power in Valence, will plant five hundred birches from Holland, two hundred plane trees and three hundred poplars from Italy on that extremly ugly shore. But first a man must be able to see ugliness, and this presupposes a knowledge of the beautiful. I have never forgotten the banks of the Elbe in Dresden. The top of the mountain of Crussol which stands out against the sky so clearly after sunset is just as hideous.

And yet if I were condemned to live in Valence, I would find lodgings in one of those fields that rise forty feet above the suspension bridge. There you are only four minutes from the theater and the center of town. The quarter of Saint-Nicolas, through which one drives to Romans and Grenoble is, like the Saunière quarter, one very long, wide street. There are even a few scraggly mulberry trees in the wide space between the street and the walls. Imagine how it would look if the Allées de Meilhan were there! This is a pretty place and all it needs is a prefect with as much imagination in 1838 as Monsieur de Meilhan had in 1789.

To give a little dignity to this Place aux Clercs, I would like to see a statue of Napoleon as second-lieutenant placed here. Those ideas that, in 1789, were current at Madame de Colombier's and in the social world of Valence, having lodged in the head of a great man who was occupied with other matters, prevented him from giving the monarchy a good second edition that would find admirers. I believe there should

*Valence: the Cathedral*

not be any nobility other than the Legion of Honor, but then, make way for those nobles! I am delighted that Waterloo has made short shrift of all the pettiness we had in us. Look at the literature of the Empire! Now Europe entrusts us with the function of *thinking for her;* hence the Belgian forgeries which keep certain highly placed personages[44] from sleeping.

Fortunately for the traveler, clubs do not predominate in Valence as they do in Tarascon and Avignon; as a result there are two reading rooms. I wasted my time in one of them, reading all sorts of trash. On looking at my watch I was annoyed and I was also annoyed in Tarascon at being dependent for all mental nourishment on the *National* which, by profession, finds that everything is going badly.

[44] The kings.

*Appendix*

# Additional Notes
## on My Travels in 1838

### [*March, 1838*]

March 11th arrived in Bordeaux. April 11th, first day of summer. Need for awnings in front of the shops. They are open at the sides to let people pass under them. Dark shadows of the noonday sun—unknown in Paris. Yesterday, Monsieur Brun's funeral. I went to Saint André's. In the evening I examined the copy of *Esprit des Lois* that Montesquieu gave Monsieur B's father, apparently in 1748.

I have not opened this book since Paris and I shall not open it for a long time. I am too lazy to write. However, I am doing a long article on Bordeaux, the counterpart of my article on Lyons but better: a descriptive tour with no extraneous reflections added. The reader knows the traveler, that is to say, the fraction $\frac{M}{N}$ by which I must multiply all his assertions.

April 7th, journey to La Brède with M.S.

### [Bordeaux, *March 15, 1838*. Morale]

That good, excellent Monsieur de Cheverus has died of grief over the tricks his priests played on him. They tossed anonymous letters over his garden walls. Monsieur Donnat, a cold man who knows the world, pays no attention to the malicious deeds of underlings.

The rage for railroads has broken out in Bordeaux as everywhere else. They are going to run a railroad from Bordeaux to the head of Buch and, once the road is built, they will be in a fine pickle to find anything to run over it. Buch produces only *royans*, excellent little fish rather like sardines.

Business is slow in Bordeaux. Only those firms that made their fortune in the past do any business today and they confine themselves in general to deals that are certain to be successful.

Love reigns in Bordeaux. It is not unusual for a married woman to leave husband and children and elope to Paris with her lover. Men's lives are separate from women's, a situation which, they say, stirs the imagination. If a man went to the same house three times in a month, public opinion would shout from the roof tops that he was paying court to the mistress of that house. Public opinion is neither too liberal nor too conservative. In general people follow the judgment of the government.

Ball, Friday, March 15.

Business: 905,000 francs in 1837.

Women are still fashionable in Bordeaux.

Climate of Bordeaux very inferior to the climate of Marseilles. Weather rainy and disagreeable again today (March 16th) caused by the west wind.

Wines.

Learning to know the wines of Bordeaux is no small matter. I like this art because it rules out any hypocrisy. You are shown a bottle of wine; not only must you name its vintage, but you must even indicate the year in which it was harvested. If you make a mistake twice in succession, you are done for. M. sold a cask of two thousand bottles for which he received fifteen hundred francs.

The priests have just put a stop to a charity ball, which was to have taken place on March 16th, by preaching against the ball without having first made the slightest move to approach the ladies on the committee.

### [Beginning of the article on customs]

In 1738, an era when France shone brilliantly in the world of thought, it was perhaps Bordeaux's way of doing things that made it inferior. In an ambitious era in which hypocrisy is useful in all careers, the character of the Bordelais which has remained frank and open, may perhaps entitle him to the first place in France.

### [La Brède]

I have a great admiration for Montesquieu and the day when I saw La Brède marked a high point in my life. There everything has a flavor of antiquity, the reverse of sensual delights.

The portrait of the woman said to be M.'s mistress, and which is still in his bedroom, has a walnut frame, not a gilded or painted frame. This rather dark room which has only one window, though fairly large and facing south, is paneled in walnut. Light walnut, not at all gloomy, but by no means imposing, is used to form little panels the size of a pane of glass.

The bed, covered with very faded green damask (M. died . . . years ago, in 1751) is supported by four heavy round walnut posts.

There is no parquet, but a plain flooring, no mirror on the mantel-piece, which is large and baronial; the shelf is four to five feet high. But the jamb on the right is worn by Montesquieu's slipper, for he was in the habit of writing on his knee.

Dom Devienne's history tells us that Montesquieu lived in La Brède from 17 . . . to 17 . . . and that he wrote *La Grandeur des Romains* there.

### [Road from Toulouse to Agen, *March 29*]

Agen. "They would be proud if they had something like this in Paris."

Trees as far as Grisolles; after that dislike of trees expressed by the owner of Castelsarrasin.

The conservative nobleman of Castelsarrasin. The South sacrificed to the North. He is afraid of everything, of expenses as well as of profits. Moreover he lies when he insists that he came from Montauban by the same coach in four hours, in other words (on the right of the Tarn) at four leagues an hour. (Describe this character.)

Exhaustion from seven to nine. Funny garrulous old woman. Competency. Glad to question her.

At Agen, I went to the café south of the coach. Read two newspapers from the 26th of March . . . ; Touching delight. Mention this.

Ownership of land. Château de Pompignan sold only a few years ago to Monsieur de Lapanouze. In Toulouse, an officer, satisfied with his lot in life, said: "Everyone despises everyone else, but no one says so to your face."

"Agreed. That has been true ever since Waterloo, since the reign of hypocrisy."

Information given by the landowner: almost everything made of brick. I went to Toulouse, to a manufacturer of those bricks. In the country: one hundred bricks, five francs, but they're throwing them away.

Road from Toulouse to Agen, March 29, in the morning; left at nine o'clock.

Monsieur Balarens, owner of the Château de Castelnau lives in Toulouse.

From Toulouse to Castelnau we traveled over an ugly barren plain.

From Castelnau, beautiful view at a tremendous distance of the Pyrenees chain covered with snow. But in spite of that it is easy to distinguish the peaks.

Saint-Jory: first change of horses. Ugly, flat country; mud walls, bad air, lack of trees, brick houses. Left Toulouse at ten minutes past nine; arrived at Saint-Jory at half-past ten.

From Toulouse to the Château de Castelnau, you travel over the plain that lies between the Garonne and the long, flat hill that runs northward forming a spur to the east. Halfway up that hill, the homely chateau. Hôtel de France at Agen (Balarens).

In Toulouse I did not see the *Illustres* of the Capitole or the Duc de Montmorency's cell. The Capitole is hopelessly ugly. The only remedy is to move it twenty feet forward, give it a new façade and put up a front of columns copied from old *Procuratie*.

Canal du Midi Riquet. In 1804 consignments estimated at ten thousand; now forty thousand. Tariffs too high. The quintal costs twenty sous from one end of the canal to the other.

From Castelnau to Castelsarrasin the road runs to the east of the Garonne.

They say *Tar* and not *Tarne*.

Office of clerk of court in Castelsarrasin bought twenty thousand; worth twenty-five hundred. Court of first instance brings in eighteen hundred . . .

Agen. Arrived in Agen the 29th at five minutes past seven.

Left Toulouse this morning at a quarter past nine. Skirted the beautiful village of Grisolles which runs along the Garonne with tall trees at the harbor.

At Valence, a portico and a covered promenade.

At Agen a street with porticoes on both sides as in Bologna; the townspeople groan about it and consider them very unsightly.

Square *canne:* 220 ft. by 16 inches thick, 140.

Bricks: the square *canne*, 3 meters; 3 m., 2250 mm. 15 inches long;

10 inches wide, 2 inches thick, 5 francs the hundred.

Dividing the land into small holdings has resulted in excellent crops from Toulouse to Agen.

The brickmakers allow the bricks to dry, a mistake the prefect should correct by public notices.

Canal du Midi: one franc the quintal from the Garonne to Cette by the Riquet canal. In 1804 new consignments at ten thousand to forty thousand francs.

Departure from Toulon in the direction of Agen. Save for a few poplars, there is not a tree thirty feet high. What a difference in the appearance it would make if there were a stand of those handsome oaks from the Val d'Arno in Tuscany! Country flat and ugly.

In Agen, Café de la Comédie.

Arrive in Pompignan at 11:30. Tall chateau beside the church, just as in Castelnau; belongs to Monsieur de Lapanouze.

Detached dovecotes in the country. Some of them are joined on to the houses.

The main road overlooks the square.

Place Lafayette. Radial ellipse. They want to paint it gray. There should be a statue in the center.

Should they try to repair the façade of the Capitole? They should copy the *Procuratie Vecchie* on the right of Saint Mark's Square, with the main structure one-quarter in advance on the total line of the building.

## [Grisolles]

Two years ago the Pompignan family sold it to Monsieur de Lapanouze. Very fertile land. The unusually early warmth of March and April brings out the buds which are then nipped by late frosts. The North does not suffer from the inconvenience of premature warmth.

First-quality hectare: twenty-four hundred francs.

Fourth class, eight hundred francs the hectare.

The poorest brick: five francs a hundred.

Well-burned brick: eight francs.

Carved brick: eight.

In Toulouse.

Well-burned bricks: sixteen francs.

Carved bricks: sixteen . . .
Molded burned bricks or burned bricks for wall arrises at fifteen inches. Square *canne*, two hundred twenty bricks.

[*Tuesday, April 17 at 5 o'clock*]
At half-past four I returned from my trip to Spain. Left Bayonne at 7:45; at ten I saw Saint-Jean-de-Luz. No adjoining walls, each house is separated from its neighbor by at least a foot of space; there should be no danger of fires here.

April 19th. Left Bayonne for Pau at five o'clock. Front seat in the compartment: eight francs.

Hôtel Saint-Etienne . . . *l'altro*, twelve francs fifty: three nights, one dinner, one supper, one coffee. Room, one franc fifty. American coffee. Very obliging waiter.

A second-hand bookseller who lives in Bayonne.

[Pau]
Conversation at the table d'hôte in Pau not nearly so dull as at the hotel in Bayonne. There was only one traveling salesman, cutting his bread with assurance and acting as if he owned the place.

2. There were three courteous men.
3. A gay old gentleman.
4. They had a good time talking.
5. One genuine ass; each of these characters well defined.

Conversation turned on yesterday's meeting of the Philharmonic Society. The poor devils are still singing *La Juive* and doing double trills on the high E string. At 204 leagues from Paris this is the extreme wave of the movement inspired by the vanity that makes the rich and the nouveau riche flock to Monsieur Robert's opera. (They say that M.S. is putting on an opera for Italian singers who can prove they have been driven out of Italy.)

[Carcassonne]
Church of Carcassonne.
Aristocratic city, admirable little church.
Transept on the left; Saint John's chapel. Inside, toward the east, three life-sized statues.

Two detached pillars near the organ.

Latin cross; one enters by a little door at the north.

Three naves, the one in the middle very wide.

First, third and fifth quadrilateral pillars with attached columns on bases the width of the nave.

Second and fourth pillars are round.

Up high at the top of the church all five pillars on each side have the beginning of an attached column. Arches in the main nave slightly pointed. Arches in small naves semicircular.

The crosspieces are much more elegant. The lattices in the apse are slightly Gothic. Large stained glass windows. Beautiful rose windows at the end of the lattices. Toward the apse a single row of pillars in the lattices.

From north to south toward the two walls two of those crosspieces are round. Three rows of pillars east of the lattices. The two nearest the church walls are round and very slender.

Very well proportioned but indistinct bas-relief in the chapel near the second pillar to the left (near the first round pillar). Two and a half feet by two and a half feet. If one understood it, this bas-relief could be used as an inscription.

On the left, near that rather barbarous sort of separation, there seem to be men in armor. On the two pillars nearest the altar are four statues covered by little canopies (pinnacles, I think).

Romanesque nave, I should say: choir and two tiers of lattices on the east, north and south, very light Gothic. Mediocre but touching painting. The saint who is being buried and is being carefully lowered into his tomb, is headless and his really beautiful head lies on one side in the foreground of the painting.

The paintings around the choir are very touching.

Below the statues, an elephant, very well carved.

The girl, who was sweeping the church, pointed out the bas-relief on the left of the entrance.

The light Gothic pillars east of the lattices are held up by a great number of iron bars. There are twelve statues in the choir at the foot of the little pillars between the windows. The first two statues on the right and on the left are placed against the pillars at the windows. All the statues, fifteen feet high, are as usual religious and very well exe-

cuted; fish, elephant, birds, peacocks and Noah's dove are not so good.
Deer, wild boar, tortoise, a very good head and at the back of the apse,
the phoenix.

I have never before seen this double row of pillars on the east of
transepts.

Birds were singing in the church where they have innocently built
their nests.

Young girl, sweeping near some children who were playing . . .
companions.

### [Carcassonne, *Saturday, April 28*]

Weather gloomy and cold; arrived yesterday at 9:30 in the evening.
Saint Nazaire's is said to have a Romanesque nave and a Gothic choir.

Saint Vincent's cathedral.

Ancient Carcassonne on a mountain alongside of the new town. As
one comes out through the gate of the new Carcassonne, the ancient
city on a height surrounded by its gray walls, very gray itself in the
midst of fresh greenery, made a good impression on me. It looks like a
city one sees in paintings.

Very pleasant boulevard. Leaving the new town I went to ancient
Carcassonne; seven rows of trees. Gate faces east. First arch in the gate
is semicircular; second and third are ogival arches. Half of the rooms
. . . in the same style as the gates of Florence.

### [Marseilles]

If Bordeaux is obviously the most beautiful city in France, Paris being
still the most adorned, Marseilles is the prettiest. The view of the sea
from La Tourette, (which can easily live down the disrepute into
which it has fallen and become fashionable), and the charming boulevards inside the city exuding coolness in the midst of such extreme
heat, make it the second most beautiful city in France. Perhaps Nantes
would rank third.

(Fine idea about sympathy, May 27th, on my way to the museum
and the review on the Allées de Meilhan. Impossible to get into the
Mass.)

May 27th, I am overcome by the number of things I have to say. I
dictated fifty pages.

Italians. Madame Mariani, crazy but pleasant. Madame Gariboldi perhaps; slow, ugly, unpleasant, shrill. Her shrieking, which they call a voice, was applauded in Marseilles. Good bit of nonsense heard this evening at the Café des Milles-Colonnes.

I don't like any part of the *Furioso*. The Belisaire tragedy to the life. The second act even more boring than the first.

Fairly large crowd at these Italians. Never a full house, my neighbor told me. Always the same faces. That witty little man, who looks like Monsieur Labaume, is always in the orchestra with a woman to whom he talks intimately in a loud tone of voice. He has a self-satisfied air which is dignified by his grave and formal demeanour. A serious-minded couple . . .

My seat is always next to theirs.

The bird that flies to Cartagena.

Olive trees that did not freeze in 1820.

The green mountain.

The runaway stagecoach.

Chapel.

Olive tree six feet high.

The alarm.

The main road from seven to 11:45 as far as Draguignan.

The driver who kept rambling on.

Mademoiselle Suzanne. I speak well enough, but I can't manage to understand.

May I come up?

The father is a very polite employee. No trouble in finding a room there, nothing but courtesy and good manners.

At midnight to the widow Boivin's.

Cash in Cannes.

At four o'clock on the 21st, twenty francs + 11 francs.

Twelve francs left to return from here to Marseilles.

| | |
|---|---|
| Tonight | 1 franc 50 |
| Dinner | 2. 50 |
| Tips | 0. 50 |
| | 4 francs 50 |

Return trip: eight francs or seven francs fifty to
go from here to Marseilles.

| | |
|---|---|
| Tuesday dinner | 2 francs 50 |
| Wednesday dinner | 2.     50 |
| | 5 francs |

Three francs left for breakfast.
Calculation of distances.
I took the other route:

| | |
|---|---|
| From Toulon to Luc | 9 hours |
| From Luc to Draguignan | 4 |
| From Draguignan to Grasse | 9 |
| | 22 hours |

Allowing for the same distance, if I leave Cannes Tuesday at six
o'clock, I shall be in Luc on Wednesday at four o'clock in the morning
and, if we leave there at once, I shall be in Toulon at one o'clock on
Wednesday and in Marseilles on Thursday. But they say that from
Cannes I should be in Luc at ten o'clock Tuesday evening, in Toulon
Wednesday and in Marselles on Thursday. But they say that from
o'clock in Marseilles.

### [*May 30, 1838*]

I saw Avignon again in three hours and a half. Therefore I was happy
from half past two till six. Notre-Dame des Doms which. . . . The
Palace: I was entranced by Giotto's window. The museum seemed
empty to me, but the joke is that it was empty of Madame de Grignan.
I cannot have imagined those eyes I saw—and shall continue to see.
Some honest director, a noble or devout man, must have smuggled her
away.

### [Basle, *June 27, 1838*]

I see in the *Constitutionel* of Sunday, June 24th, that . . . was able to
appear on Tuesday, the 26th. Nantes is mentioned, but the details are
suppressed and the article is misspelled and signed in a false handwriting
with a false name. What struck me particularly was the aversion of
those gentlemen to details. Apparently the readers of the *Constitutionel*
find them difficult to grasp.

On June 28th, after seeing the cathedral, I went to the Natural History Museum. July 7th, see Aix-la-Chapelle. . . .

Must see the *Constitutionel* of the 26th: death of General Haxo and the publication of *Mémoires d'un Touriste* on the 26th.

June 27th. By spending two or three days in each town the trip becomes absorbing. You notice the same qualities in different objects. For example, comfort at an inn or the beauty of a town. This might be a good way for children, whose attention span is short, to travel. What seems to be stupidity is often merely a lack of that faculty.

### [*June 27, 1838*]

The German. A visit of twenty-four hours in the Hôtel des Gentils-hommes in Berne is equivalent to a trip to Germany or at least a summary of such a trip: genial good nature, attentiveness, zeal and eagerness to give you the paper, the time, etc. . . . These people have a passion for pleasing the traveler and making him comfortable—and all for six francs fifty.

At Basle I was sorry I had not gone from Berne to Neuchâtel. If I do not go to Dresden from Frankfurt, perhaps I shall regret it when I get back to Paris.

So then, the German: (1) meticulous, painstaking people; (2) lack the courage to omit details for the sake of clarity.

### [Basle, *June 27–28, 1838*]

German people are meticulous about the cleanliness of their towns and their inns. The German does not have the courage to neglect details.

Three times I picked up the sailing list from Strasbourg (Kehl) to Cologne (printed in three languages) for June, 1838, and three times I put it down impatiently.

The German cannot bring himself to begin the list with six clear lines. For example:

Three different boats run from Strasbourg to Cologne.

The first boat makes the trip in forty-eight hours, leaves Strasbourg at such and such an hour, costs. . . .

The second boat takes forty-eight hours, leaves . . . costs. . . .

The third boat takes sixty hours, leaves . . . costs. . . .

Those six clear lines would be enough for most travelers, but I have not been able to extract them from the enormous printed sheet they call a timetable.

### [*1838*]

In Aubagne, the . . . I saw that *this book* was about to appear. In Basle I see in the *Constitutionel* of June 26th that it is to appear today, the day of Queen Victoria's coronation. *Idea of the 23rd of June, 1837,* in Le Havre. In Rotterdam the 10th of July, *Constitutionel* of the 8th, second edition . . .

I read it over again in the evening. Basle, the 28th of June. Momentary boredom which ends only at page 51. There is a great deal of description in the beginning, but the content is not very interesting. Soon the reader exclaims: *Raphael, ubi es?* Around page 51, you say: the author has aged. Miss Rose Esterhazy's typewriter might really have stirred up the first part as far as page 25.

It needed the story of Miss Rose Esterhazy's typewriter changing the name after the Norman's bargain with the man from the Dauphiné. This is what I was told this evening at the house of a charming woman whose wit is such that one forgives her husband's many millions.

July 1st in Strasbourg I received two letters from Colomb telling me about the contract with Laroche and saying that he has delivered the second volume which should have arrived—797 pages in all.

### [Strasbourg, *July 1, 2, 3, 1838*]

I saw the Münster, Saint Thomas's church, the new temple and the strange dance of the dead, five great pieces.

Not one big tree in Strasbourg. Wide streets, large wooden houses; on their steep roofs, three rows of dormer windows. This is what one sees from three sides of the parade ground; the fourth side overlooks the square.

The Royal Palace, a building in dark stone, not at all handsome; the archbishopry equally lacking in beauty. Strasbourg is perhaps the one city in France where there are less decent houses. But the streets are broad and it will be easy to make asphalt pavements.

The Ill, a nasty little river with dirty waters, runs through Strasbourg and is even divided into several branches—humidity. Strasbourg is unaware of the Rhine.

It is a strange river; the little branches that surround the main stream form an endless number of islands . . . the *thalweg*, the mid-channel downstream. Ever since the 1st at noon, *io soffro di si.* . . .

Strasbourg, July 2nd. I answered letters from di Fiori, Kol. Have had little hot weather since . . . in Geneva.

The evening in Geneva . . . by the children in a large. . . .

Boy's charming face, young girl of sixteen is utterly charming.

### [*July 2, 1838*. Dance of the Dead]

Strasbourg, new temple, five charming pictures belonging to a dance of the dead. Figure No. 2 (coming from the organ on the right towards the left) perfectly clear. Movement, figures of women. . .

### [Strasbourg, *July 3, 1838*]

It is raining and I curse the mail for not bringing me the second volume that Colomb says he mailed on June 23rd.

And the Church triumphs in actual fact at this moment.

I'm afraid this book may be too concise in style; its real emptiness horrifies me.

This will have the defect of . . . *hard to read*, without having the great excuse of merit.

The tale of the Russian Princess Samoïloff consoles me a little. It is not too concise.

Tomorrow I count on going to Basle, Mainz, Frankfurt, Rotterdam, Amsterdam, Brussels by way of Antwerp and, around July 20th, to Paris.

### [*July 11*. Rotterdam, *July 10 and 11, 1838*]

The best strawberries of the year, vastly superior to the strawberries in Marseilles. Here they take the trouble to cultivate them. I saw the fruit on sale here.

Tremendous heat around July 11th.

Yesterday, the 10th, in the *Constitutionel* of the 8th, they mention a second edition.

A knavish trick!

The waiter in B . . . had counted the florins on the table; but when he received my napoleon and realized my ignorance, he said: "The napoleon is worth nine florins," and he filched one of them. I saw the trick; the honest and honorable delegate owed . . . ten florins. But I would not swear to this before the Sorbonne, although sure of my nine. A napoleon worth ten florins!

If Monsieur de la D . . . brings up this matter of the . . . asks me for ten Dutch florins more, on the 20th I shall be in France. The napoleon is worth only nine florins and a half.

Two omissions on p. 271, the court, and on p. 294, Grignan. Wrote to Kolo from Amsterdam on July 12th.

July 16th, 1838 at Groot, awaiting permission promised for this morning, but which has not yet come, and perhaps will not come tomorrow. I feel as though I am in a prison.

Monsieur Herman, junior, husband of the imperious woman with no neck and black eyebrows on the steamer from Ilsesheim to Bingen (I think). The bayonet thrust.

July 16th, 1838, waiting for permission, Groot. 289 La Bruyère. Comment: a man protected by a . . . must be more of an imbecile . . . than another.

### [*July 16, '38 Groot*]

394. I regret the money. I have a horror of thievery which will make traitors in the next war.

[45]August 3rd, 1838. *She gives things the amica of eleven year. Beginning in 1827.*

August 4th, 1838. The people around an author admire him too much or too little. True for Dominque. On August 4th, 1838, he wrote to M.

[45] This is Stendhal's English as he wrote it in this diary. (Translator's note)

Distances covered in the 1838 journey; left Paris March 8th, returned to Paris July 22nd, 1838 (135 days to the 16th). I do not count the stages between relays.

| | | |
|---|---|---|
| From Paris to Bordeaux | 155 | leagues by coach |
| From Bordeaux to Toulouse | 64 | " " " |
| Return | 64 | " " " |
| From Bordeaux to Bayonne | 53 | " " " |
| From Bayonne to Saint-Jean-de-Luz | 6 | " " " |
| From Saint-Jean-de-Luz to la Bidassoa | 2 | " " " |
| In Spain | 2 | " " " |
| From Bidassoa to Saint-Jean-de-Luz | 2 | " " " |
| From Saint-Jean-de-Luz to Bayonne | 6 | " " " |
| From Bayonne to Pau | 25 | " " " |
| From Pau to Tarbes | 10 | " " " |
| From Tarbes to Auch | 17 | " " " |
| From Auch to Toulouse | 17 | " " " |
| From Toulouse to Carcassonne | 23 | " " " |
| From Carcassonne to Narbonne | 15 | " " " |
| From Narbonne to Montpellier by way of Béziers and Mèze | 25 | " " " |
| From Montpellier to Nîmes | 13 | " " " |
| From Nîmes to Arles | 7 | " " " |
| From Arles to Marseilles by the canal | | |

(By sea from Marseilles to Arles, by land from Arles to Tarascon I follow the estimates of the coach company.)

From Marseilles to Tarascon          28
From Tarascon to Valence
From Valence to Grenoble          23
From Grenoble to Chambéry
From Chambéry to Geneva
From Geneva to Villeneuve (by steamer)

*Return*
From Geneva to Berne
From Berne to Basle
From Basle to Strasbourg by way of Freiburg
From Strasbourg to Baden
From Pont de Baden, Ilsezheim to Mannheim
From Mannheim to Cologne
From Cologne to Rotterdam
From Rotterdam to Amsterdam
From Amsterdam to The Hague
From The Hague to Huningen and return
From The Hague to Delft
From Delft to Rotterdam
From Rotterdam to Mordyck (by steamer)
From Mordyck to Breda
From Breda to Grootzundert
From Grootzundert to Antwerp
From Antwerp to Brussels (railroad)
From Brussels to Paris by way of Cambrai, Péronne and Pont-Sainte-Maxence

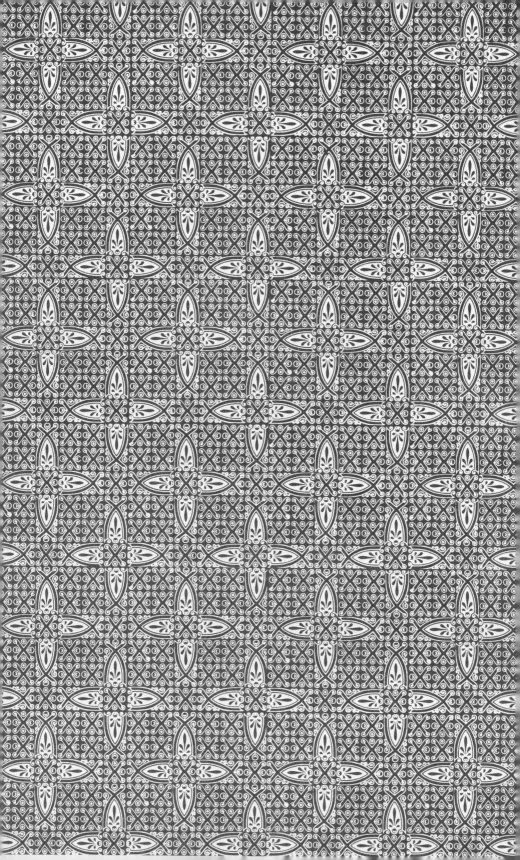